The tragic vision of Joyce Carol Oates

The tragic vision
of Joyce Carol Oates

Mary Kathryn Grant

Duke University Press

Durham, N. C.   1978

Contents

Preface

The inspiration for this study occurred over seven years ago at the spring Modern Literature meeting at East Lansing, Michigan. At that time, I had the pleasure of meeting Joyce Carol Oates. Although we have not met again since, despite the fact that for many years only the Detroit River separated us as Ms. Oates taught at the University of Windsor and I at Mercy College of Detroit, Ms. Oates has been gracious enough to correspond with me and to grant permission to quote from her works. For this I am most grateful.

Few things of importance can be accomplished alone. This book, therefore, has existence because of the support of a number of people and it is to them that it is dedicated. Firstly, my friends at Indiana University whose assistance was far-reaching; particular gratitude and affection belong to Dr. and Mrs. Robert Gray Gunderson, whose friendship and intellectual stimulation enlivened and enriched the years during which this book was progressing. Mr. Anthony Shipps of the Indiana University Library and Dr. James H. Justus of the English Department also offered many ideas, much encouragement, and helpful materials.

My family, friends, and community also deserve special thanks, in particular Dr. Sheila O'Brien, B.V.M., Dr. Emily George, R.S.M., and Molly Macy, R.S.M.

I would like to acknowledge the role Mrs. Joanna Hitchcock of Princeton University Press played in helping this study reach this stage. Mrs. Joanne Ferguson of Duke University Press has been especially kind and a pleasure to work with.

Finally, because I not only recognize but also am very sympathetic with the concern that women be recognized uniquely and particularly, I tried to eliminate the use of he, him, and his when I meant humankind. The havoc these efforts produced in the rhetoric, however, was unbearable. Therefore, I have resorted to the conventional use of the masculine.

Mt. St. Mary's College
Los Angeles

Abbreviations

Throughout this study, the following editions of the works of Joyce Carol Oates have been used. All citations are noted in the text, prefixed by the appropriate abbreviations.

AF   *Angel Fire* (Baton Rouge, La.: Louisiana State University Press, 1973)

AS   *Anonymous Sins and Other Poems* (Baton Rouge, La.: Louisiana State University Press, 1969)

DWM   *Do With Me What You Will* (New York: Vanguard Press, 1973)

EOI   *The Edge of Impossibility: Tragic Forms in Literature* (New York: Vanguard Press, 1972)

EP   *Expensive People* (New York: Vanguard Press, 1968)

GED   *A Garden of Earthly Delights* (New York: Vanguard Press, 1967)

G   *The Goddess and Other Women* (New York: Vanguard Press, 1974)

HG   *The Hungry Ghosts: Seven Allusive Comedies* (Los Angeles: Black Sparrow Press, 1974)

MI   *Marriages and Infidelities* (New York: Vanguard Press, 1972)

NHNE   *New Heaven, New Earth* (New York: Vanguard Press, 1974)

S   *The Seduction and Other Stories* (Los Angeles: Black Sparrow Press, 1975)

them   *them* (New York: Vanguard Press, 1969)

W   *Wonderland* (Greenwich, Conn.: Fawcett, Crest, 1971)

This is the author's preferred edition; it represents a revision
of the hard-cover edition published by Vanguard Press, 1971.

WSF   *With Shuddering Fall* (New York: Vanguard Press, 1964)

Joyce Carol Oates frequently uses ellipses in her writings. Where the
use of unspaced periods appears to deviate from the *MLA Style Sheet*
in citations, this may be assumed to be the author's own style.

The tragic vision of Joyce Carol Oates

ONE

A theory of art

1

In a literary era which variously proclaims the death of the novel, a reversion to fantasy and romance, and the evolution of prose narrative to the nonfiction novel, Joyce Carol Oates maintains a posture of defiance, insisting that the novel is not dead and that art, specifically prose fiction, can and does help to give some shaping order to our reality. The pages of her novels are filled with the inchoate, the "fantastically real"—murder, suicide, riot, rape, loss of identity, loss of community—yet out of this violence a tragic affirmation struggles to emerge, the hope of a hope. "Writing fiction today," she attests in her speech accepting the National Book Award for her novel *them*, "sometimes seems an exercise in stubbornness and an anachronistic gesture that goes against the shrill

[3]

demands of the age—that only the present has meaning, that the contemplative life is irrelevant, that only the life of purest sensation is divine, and that the act of giving shape to sensation, of giving permanence to the present, is somehow an inversion of the life principle itself."[1] Oates refuses to side with those writers who insist that the novel has lost its power to interpret life; on the contrary, she firmly believes in the "power of narrative fiction to give coherence to jumbled experience and to bring about a change of heart."[2] This is not to say she writes simplistic or moralistic fables, nor that she seeks to superimpose order on the disordered world of which she writes. Her fiction, infused with her vision of the "tragically diminished urban world,"[3] nudges the reader toward a new consciousness.

A writer trying to make sense of this "mysterious age, the present," Oates insists, is also creating the age. "The writer of prose is committed to re-creating the world through language," she argues. "The opposite of language is silence; silence for human beings is death." Her fiction is her attempt to "give a shape to certain obsessions of mid-century Americans—a confusion of love and money, of categories of public and private experience, of a demonic urge . . . an urge to violence as the answer to all problems, an urge to self-annihilation, suicide, the ultimate experience and the ultimate surrender. The use of language is all we have to pit against death and silence."[4] This testament to the power of art underlines her awesome sense of the responsibility of the writer who, by raising the consciousness of the age, creates history and the future.

So insistent is she that "all art is moral, educative, illustrative," that she dismisses her fourth novel, Wonderland, as immoral because she could not resolve its moral issues.[5] Art, she insists, demands a vision of life as cyclical tragedy, and its purpose is to lead the reader to a more profound "sense of the mystery and the sanctity of the human predicament."[6] For a work not to achieve this is for it to be judged a moral failure. Her present body of fiction tells the tragic tale of a decade wasted by war, assassinations, and riots, and a people paralyzed by their fear of being powerless to change things. But her works do more than merely chronicle the horrors of the sixties and early seventies; they are efforts to raise the consciousness of ordinary people to the realization of the destruction of their lives, to "show us how to get through and transcend pain,"[7] to encourage us to continue the struggle to put some meaning into human life.

Her works stand as a refutation of David Goldknopf's contention that "conventional reality cannot support the serious contemporary novel . . . [it produces] too coarse-grained, embarrassed, perfunctory case studies and a social environment preempted by other media."[8] The alternatives Goldknopf sees are capitulations to realism or to fantasy, and where he would deem the task of the modern novel to soften the facts of harsh reality, Oates boldly presents these facts for the twofold purpose of raising the consciousness of her readers and of urging them on to the goal of affirmation and celebration of life. She does, in fact, seem to possess the "original mind" Goldknopf seeks which can discover the "stress lines along which the present will surrender to the future." She further avoids the pitfall of "over-personalization of experience," which he declares the "enemy of realism."[9] She does indeed disprove the fear that there can be no serious contemporary novel.

Oates's works also stand apart from the countertrend of turning to fantasy and romance. In his study of the fiction of the 1960s, *Beyond the Wasteland*, Raymond Olderman discusses this movement toward romance. He characterizes the decade as possessing a "growing sense of the mystery of fact itself and a loss of confidence in our own power to effect change and to control events," which he argues leads to the creation of contemporary versions of romance. Obviously with her insistence on reality, Joyce Carol Oates does not shrink from "rendering the actual texture of human experience."[10]

The mystery and sanctity of the human predicament is a crucial concept in Oates's fiction—not easily rendered in the "rhetoric of moral certainty."[11] In fact more often rendered in ambiguity and uncertainty, her fiction is not mimetic; she seeks not simply to record the "fabulous reality" of the twentieth century but to offer a vision of life, life that is incomplete and often tragic. The first step to a change of heart must be a change of consciousness, a heightened awareness of one's tragic plight. In describing contem-

[5]

porary fiction, Ihab Hassan astutely comments, "the pursuit of love brings men to the threshold of mystical experience and the search for freedom brings them to the frontiers of nihilism: thus saintliness and crime violently merge in the quest of new consciousness."[12] At the heart of Oates's fiction is the violent coming together of love and freedom from which emerges a new consciousness.

Oates keenly experiences the dilemma Philip Roth discusses when he writes of the problem the contemporary author has in confronting and making sense of his times. Roth notes: "The American writer in the middle of the twentieth century has his hands full in trying to understand and then describe, and then make *credible* much of the American reality. It stupefies, it sickens, it infuriates, and finally it is even a kind of embarrassment to one's meager imagination. The actuality is continually outdoing our talents and the culture tosses up figures almost daily that are the envy of any novelist."[13] If some of Oates's fiction seems incredible, it is because she unflinchingly describes American reality, a reality that is stranger than fiction. "America outdoes all its writers," observes the child-narrator of *Expensive People*, an observation entirely consonant with the views of the author herself.

She is, as critic Alfred Kazin notes, "attached to life by well-founded apprehensions that nothing lasts, nothing is safe, nothing is all around us."[14] Face to face with this void, she refuses to capitulate. There is about her fiction an urgent call to greater and greater consciousness of the "sickening," "stupefying," "infuriating" reality. If her works lack happy characters and happy endings, it is because "there's no need to write about happy people, happy problems; there's only the moral need to instruct readers concerning the direction to take in order to achieve happiness (or whatever: maybe they don't want happiness, only confusion)."[15]

Moreover, her fiction asks the questions raised by Saul Bellow when he writes: "Either we want life to continue or we do not. . . . If we do want it to continue . . . in what form shall life be justified?"[16] She repeatedly explores the ramifications of this question. In praising Harriette Arnow's novel *The Dollmaker*, she applauds any work which has the power to "deal with the human soul, caught

[6]

in the stampede of time, unable to gauge the profundity of what passes over it, like the characters of certain plays of Yeats who live through terrifying events but who cannot understand them; in this way history passes over most of us. Society is caught in a convulsion whether of growth or of death, and ordinary people are destroyed. They do not, however, understand that they are 'destroyed.' "[17] To this goal—awakening ordinary people to their destruction—Oates is unswervingly committed. A comment she makes about Flannery O'Connor, "no writer obsessively works and reworks a single theme that is without deep personal meaning,"[18] is equally applicable to herself; the working and reworking of the theme of destruction occurs throughout Oates's writings.

Her fiction is discomforting and starkly real. She has unshakeable faith that the human spirit can—someday—"redeem the time." "Blake, Whitman, Lawrence and others," she notes in an interview with Walter Clemons, "have had a vision of a transformation of the human spirit. I agree with it strongly myself. I think it's coming. . . . I don't think I'll live to see it. But I want to do what little I can to bring it nearer."[19] Her phenomenal body of works attests to this desire: from the early tragic tale of Karen Herz's struggle to become her own person to Elena Howe's groping efforts to achieve liberation, this theme receives her constant attention.

There is, however, a certain resignation or acceptance of life-as-it-is in some of her early works. When it is impossible to change things, she seems to say, it is perhaps best to accept them. Her voice sounds through the admonition the Grandfather gives to young Billie in "Swamps": " 'This-here is a damn good world, a goddam good world, it's all you got an' you better pay attention to it.' "[20] Not merely a supine resignedness, the advice calls for a more aggresive posture, although "paying attention" to the world does not carry the same urgent call for greater consciousness that the thrust of her later works does.

But affirmation is not easily arrived at; it cannot be a facile victory. So it is on the struggle that Oates's fiction most frequently concentrates, never surrendering the possibility of affirmation, yet never achieving it. During the interview with Walter Clemons, she con-

[7]

fesses that with *Wonderland* she had come to the end of a phase of her life. From there she would "move toward a more articulate moral position, not just dramatizing nightmarish problems but trying to show possible ways of transcending them."[21] If her first five novels are dramatizations of nightmares, *Do With Me What You Will*, written after *Wonderland*, is a transitional work; Elena Howe does try to transcend her nightmarish world, but the novel does not achieve transcendence or affirmation. It is a searching piece, belonging neither to the body of works which almost despairingly depicts the times nor to the more serious work to which she considers the former "only preliminary."[22]

Oates refuses to mitigate the anguish of arriving at affirmation. As a result, much of her early fiction seems mired in dense, sordid events. She has been accused of writing pulp fiction, of producing "too much, too quickly, . . . too little self-criticized,"[23] of "chronicling only spiritual disintegration and . . . the total loss of self."[24] Taken together, however, her body of novels yields a gradually developing growth toward affirmation—still to be arrived at. In evaluating her own work *them*, she makes specific mention of the fact that, however gruesome the narrative may be, the value of the work lies in the fact that "they [the characters] all survived."[25]

Unable to capitulate and deny what lies behind the struggle, her fiction yields the affirmation and celebration of survivors. She is in full harmony with Charles Glicksberg when he writes: "So long as life continues (and it is not to be annulled by the vision of nothingness), it must be lived, and literature, however tragic in outlook, even when it embraces the poles of extreme negation, is essentially a celebration of life."[26] Her fiction is her effort to voice a celebrative sense of life.

Not all Oates's characters are unable to see their own unhappiness for what it is. Wreszin from the short story "Ruth," for example, has sufficient aptitude to reflect on his unhappiness. He explores his situation with Ruth, the Wreszins' houseguest for the summer. "He went over and over with her the curious problem of his unhappiness. No one he had ever known had wondered about being unhappy . . . as if there were other possible states" (G 96). The mysterious possibility of being happy intrigues him; his experiential awareness has not accounted for this feeling.

When Lea Gregg unfolds her life story, her young male listener responds " 'a man that's a doctor, well a man like that . . . he, well, he's *got* to come into contact with experience. Real experience. You know . . . life and death, suffering and all that . . . and happiness, too, sometimes. . . .' " (G 127). Sometimes, happiness: an afterthought, an undreamed of, unhoped for, unexpected reality.

Unlike Kurt Vonnegut's Bokonon, who urges the creation of *foma*, "harmless truths" that "make you brave and kind and healthy and happy,"[27] Oates proffers only models of survival. She refuses to "falsify [reality] with patterns too neat, too inclusive."[28] Defending the depressing quality of *Wonderland*, she argues that the work possesses "a certain human value: it shows you how to get through."[29] Whether or not Oates moves from survival, from "getting through," to a transcendent vision is a matter that the appearance of later works will reveal. For the present it is possible to examine only the existing body of works—her novels, collections of short stories, books of poetry, books of critical essays, uncollected stories, poems, essays, plays—for the outlines and contours of that ever-developing sense of affirmation.

2

Man struggles under the triple threat of being killed by life itself, by some other person, or by oneself. At the same time, he possesses the same power to kill others. "Life is killing," Joyce Carol Oates writes in her review of *The Dollmaker*, "a killing of other people or of oneself, a killing of one's soul."[30] In this sense we are all killers, as her fiction repeatedly reminds us. In the face of this fact, we must work at being free, at living fully—as her fiction ultimately suggests.

As Saul Bellow celebrates life, the greatness and dignity of man, and the need for brotherhood, so does Joyce Carol Oates—through paradoxical contradictions. Characters "get through" life, merely survive, there is no functioning community, and man is destroyed in the Wasteland, yet the ultimate effect of the fiction is to underline the ineluctable necessity of establishing community and of affirming and celebrating life and man. Like Bellow, Oates refuses to indulge in facile and solipsistic answers, in *foma* or placebos. Neither artist turns his back on reality, on the harsh demands of twentieth-century America, and neither capitulates his vision of affirmation.

The same penetrating quest that infuses Bellow's works informs Oates's; they ask "how man may survive as a creature fully possessed of his humanity, in touch with the 'axial lines of existence,' in a tangled world." [31] The works of both artists keenly attest to the preservation of humanity and the mystery of the human predicament.

Firmly traditional, Oates stands between the opposing tendencies in modern fiction: she belongs neither to the tape-recorded, man-on-the-street realism of the nonfictionalists—Andy Warhol, Norman Mailer, and Truman Capote—nor to the "ethically controlled fantasy" [32] of the fabulators, of John Hawkes, Kurt Vonnegut, and John Barth. Nevertheless, her fiction embodies aspects of both. Her novel *them*, she declares, is a work of "history in fictional form," generously sprinkled with identifiable reality, with letters from Maureen to herself, just as her short story "Double Tragedy Strikes Tennessee Hill Family" [33] is told almost entirely through newspaper items, and *Wonderland* is interspersed throughout with newspaper clippings, headlines, and reports. In her use of realistic detail, Oates carefully skirts the danger of becoming a "supine tape-recorder novelist who registers everything and records nothing." [34]

Oates's attention to detail is almost obsessive; she painstakingly describes the sordid and depressing aspects of her characters' lives. One of the few plaudits she has received from feminist critics is based on one such detail. Susan Cornillon credits Oates as being one of the very few women writers who alludes to depilation; [35] in *them* Loretta complains about men not understanding a woman's need for razor blades. This concern for recording the trivial and inconsequential is entirely consistent with the overall thrust of Oates's works which might well be summarized thus: to force her readers to examine in detail their own lives, to discover the petty, trivial concerns which gnaw away that life.

The effect this minute scrutiny of life has on the reader is often depressing, but not so for the writer. If Oates can be taken seriously when she writes about writing, then one can conclude that she finds writing a means of transcendence. A writer in one of her short stories explains, " 'I could let it depress me, but actually writing about something is a means of transcending it . . . The writer puts everything in his writing, all the bewilderment and convolutions and despair, but he leaves out the vision of himself writing" (MI 119). This vision must necessarily be of him transcending, through the act of writing, the depressing and despairing glimpse of life.

Another way to achieve this transcendence is described ironically by Titus Skinner in Oates's drama *Miracle Play*. Skinner, a drug dealer responsible for the death of two boys and the vicious beating of a young girl, faces electrocution. He tells the audience that he has come to like the electric chair, "you know, in a crazy way . . . how you get to like something you been adjacent to for a while . . ." After he is wired seemingly for the execution, he picks up a light bulb and shores up "all the flow-through of the energies that is loose in here, an' in the universe."[36] And the bulb lights up. He achieves what Oates has described elsewhere as the "final, wordless affirmation of life" (NHNE 272), however paradoxical or ironic he may be. Skinner has lived adjacent to the chair so that when it becomes a reality in his life, he can transform it from terror to transcendence.

Another manifestation of this need for transcendence is comically depicted in the character of Nora Drexler in "Magna Mater." Nora craves order in every aspect of her world. Even as she weeds the garden, she reflects on how she hates disorder and untidiness. She perceives that she shares "with Yeats and Stevens and others of her saints a need for assertion, for staking her claims of a particularity of being in a gross universe." For her to achieve a sense of herself, staking her claim as a particular being in a "gross universe," she must assert her superiority over the weeds, over her "chubby hectic child," over all that threatens to destroy her orderly house of cards. Until her afternoon is ruined by the unexpected visit of some colleagues, she had ever so tentatively achieved that transcendence.

On the other hand, *Expensive People* reads more like a fantasy with its obvious moral overtones. Granville Hicks wryly observes that the fantastic element of the novel is clearly evident in Nada's being able to reach every number she telephones.[37] Not any more subtle is the fictive Eden County of her short stories, many of which begin with the fairy-tale opener "Some time ago in Eden County...."[38] However, the setting of Eden County does not always suggest a prelapsarian state.

The rural southern setting, the fictive county with its own families and place names, the thematic concern with the conflicts of the human heart, even some of her experiments with point of view and sense of time, have led critics to compare Joyce Carol Oates with William Faulkner. Undoubtedly certain comparisons obtain, but the similarities break down abruptly when the focus falls on the intensity of character development and portrayal and the power of the story itself. Oates has not—yet—written works with the magnitude and stature of *Absalom, Absalom!* or *Light in August* or *Go Down, Moses*. She has not yet created her own Quentin Compsons, Lena Groves, or Joe Christmases.

A strong point in her fiction is her fully realized sense of place, which leads critics to align her with Eudora Welty and Flannery O'Connor. She herself has written often on Flannery O'Connor in ways which reflect a sense of her own writing and her kinship with O'Connor. O'Connor's "real concern," she maintains, "is the revelation of a transcendental world of absolute value beyond the cheap, flashy wasteland of modern America." This revelation, however, proffers no answers, no glib solutions to the mystery of modern life; her writings are "celebrations of the fact of mystery, that is all."[39]

Oates's praise of Doris Lessing also reveals some of the deeper issues in her own writing. Noting that Lessing feels a kinship with Norman Mailer, she identifies the point of greatest similarity: "his complete identification with the era in which he lives, his desire to affect radically the consciousness of the times, to dramatize himself as a spiritual representative of the times, and its contradictions." Additionally, the American author applauds her British colleague, whose fiction is a "conscious 'creating' of a set of values by which people can live, albeit in a difficult, tragically diminished urban world."[40]

The writer with whom Oates seems to have the greatest affinity is D. H. Lawrence, not the Lawrence of blood-knowledge and understanding but the Lawrence of the perpetual fight against the dehumanization and loss of self brought on by the encroaching industrial society, the Lawrence of *Blutbruderschaft* and of community. The man who dreams that given the right conditions we could "live our lives in love," the man who is aflame with the mystery of life is a kindred spirit. She considers Lawrence at his worst when he is "stridently dogmatic, authoritative, speaking without ambiguity or mystery."[41]

Consonant with her own belief in the daily struggle to "get through" is a similar tenet in Lawrence. In her short study of the poet-novelist, *The Hostile Sun*, she notes that he "trusted himself, endured and suffered himself, worked his way through himself (sometimes only barely) and came through—'look! we have come through!'—and he expects no less of his readers."[42] An experiential knowledge of what it means to have suffered and survived and a commitment to offering a portrayal of that effort in one's writings is a strong point of affinity between the two authors.

Oates acknowledges Lawrence's denial of tragedy, based in part on the currently popular notion of the death of God. "Where to many people," she writes, "tragedy as an art form or attitude toward life might be dying because belief in God is dying, to Lawrence tragedy is impure, representative of a distorted claim to prominence in the universe, a usurpation of the Other, the Infinite."[43] While she might not agree with Lawrence's denial of tragedy, she is totally sympathetic with the belief in the death of God which leads Lawrence to denial and herself to a search for newer modes of tragic forms. She postulates in her study of tragedy that "if communal belief in God has diminished so that, as writers, we can no longer presume upon it, then a redefinition of God in terms of the furtherest reaches of man's hallucinations can provide us with a new basis for tragedy" (EOI 8).

Although Lawrence and Oates do not share a belief in tragedy, they do possess an affirming celebration of life: something they both have in common with other visionary artists. "Getting through" is the first step toward affirmation and celebration without which no further step can be contemplated. The quest for an authentic means to celebrate and affirm life, always ramified by the pressing and tragic concerns of modern society, permeates Oates's fiction—as it does that of Lawrence, Blake, Tolstoy, Faulkner, and Bellow.

The woman artist to whom Oates has the greatest similarity is Flannery O'Connor. Both writers seek to describe those experiences by which a person is jolted into a consciousness of his own situation, so that he may take his life into his own hands and give it direction. The difference, however, lies in each author's use of violence. O'Connor's characters are affected by a violence which transforms them, which refocuses their lives, or brings them to a kind of rebirth. Oates's fictive creations, on the other hand, haphazardly fall into violence which is often not only not productive or creative but often totally destructive, stripping them of what little power they had over their lives or control of its direction. They are not reborn through the violence as an O'Connor character would be but are diminished. They are often presented as pitiable creatures who serve, as it were, as warnings to us of what could happen to us unless we awaken to the plight of our lives.

Violence in O'Connor's fiction is always precipitated, while in Oates's work it is often random; it just happens. There are no entries "into the world of guilt and sorrow," no new worlds, opened hearts, or "judgment days"—just the tragic everyday existence of people unable to change their lives. Both writers deal with the same type of fictive character, the ordinary person confronting his own meanness, his smallness, his powerlessness. In O'Connor, however, he is redeemed through grace and his life is changed; in Oates, he often resignedly accepts his life-as-it-is with no hope of redemption or change.

Oates has written on O'Connor several times, in particular her poem "Firing a Field" is dedicated to the memory of Flannery O'Connor and appears in *Angel Fire* in the third section of the collection, "Revelations." The poem is addressed to unbelievers and employs the metaphor of a blazing fire which, although it destroys, also serves to "unravel the landscape." The burning is a punishment for so much sunlight, and the final effect is that "our revenge sifts downward like falling ash / mightily / upon all creation." The fiery light from O'Connor's writings sears and illumines—and in the end we are changed, another testimony to Oates's firm belief in the power of fiction and to her sensitive kinship to an artist whose basic themes are much like her own.

3

In Joyce Carol Oates's works three themes—woman, city, and community—merge into an all-too-real nightmare. Her cities are the settings for death, riots, and the violent wreckage of human lives. Her women are victims, raped physically and psychically by both men and the world. Not only is community an unrealizable dream, but few characters even aspire to it. John L'Heureux notes that her fiction "coldly calibrates the moral irresponsibility of two generations," [44] two generations of social violence, of struggling for identity and community.

The tragedy limned in Oates's works is born out of a "break between self and community, a sense of isolation" (EOI 3). It is not the tragedy of Aristotle: modern tragedy, she asserts, is without catharsis. [45] Perhaps "before catharsis" better describes her own works insofar as she fully exploits the tragic situation and then withholds catharsis. Her endings are low-keyed, often anticlimactic —a lonely woman rocking her life away in an asylum, a young girl returning to her family after her release from an asylum, parents murdered by their children—hardly high forms of tragic endings. At first glance a reader cannot but wonder whether Oates believes redemption is possible. Her characters frequently mouth bromides about love, support, and community, but nowhere in her fiction do these become reality. The phoenix image which the conclusion of *them* suggests falls short of being convincing; nothing in the previous 507 pages compels the reader to hope for a new or better life. Ironically, the very absence of love, redemption, community in her fiction, bespeaks the vital need for and belief in these realities. "We have the same hearts. We did the same thing; we are all killers, we need help; we need forgiveness." Karen screams in *With Shuddering Fall*. And in a very real way all Oates's characters are killers, all in need of forgiveness and redemption—and all unforgiven. If redemption is withheld in Oates's world, it is because she cannot lie; she cannot compromise because she knows too well that redemption, if it is reached at all, is not easily achieved.

Oates's more recent fiction tends away from straight-line narratives and touches occasionally on the metaphysical questions: what is art? what is life? what is personal identity or personality? This art-life conflict runs particularly through the stories collected in *The Goddess*, from the opening narrative of a young woman gangbanged during the shooting of a movie, who wants to know if there was really film in the camera, to the cerebral ruminations in "Magna Mater," of the woman who persistently argues that life does not grow out of ordinary, routine, emotional life but from "a higher consciousness altogether!" She also contends with blatant arch-superiority that certainly art is the "possession of a very few" and has nightmares that "our universities will be vulgarized, destroyed . . . our programs infested with grotesque 'literature' . . . even illiterate work." A purist craving the traditional, the recognized and established, she argues elitism—and realism. Her words and her life are at odds.

Art, Oates affirms, is mimetic; it imitates life as well as art. In a number of short stories and at least in one poem, Oates has initiated earlier works and endeavored to write second versions of familiar stories. Her poem, "Women in Love" (AS 62–63), derivative of

[16]

D. H. Lawrence's novel by the same title, speaks of drowning, of love "running its way / to earth." The tone and mood of the poem are Lawrencian. She writes of "silence simple / as a finger / upon a string / to still all vibration: / a man's touch." The image of the touch of love being able to still and quiet all vibrations strongly evokes the theme of the novel, as the metaphor of love running into the earth, "to mineral, earth's bone," suggests the novelist's concern for the exploitation of the earth. Even the ambiguity of the concluding lines "Love never flows / to any form" is reminiscent of some of the unresolved issues of Lawrence's work.

In "The Metamorphosis," Matthew, a strong, healthy husband and father, a car salesman, with a birthday approaching, has a dream which frightens him into a state of withdrawal and eventually to hospitalization—not unlike Gregor of Kafka's story. In an essay on Kafka, Oates observes that Gregor's transcendence takes place not within him but exterior to him—in the person of his sister. And she reads in his sister's act a "wordless, affirmation of life that Gregor . . . could not make," an act of "metamorphosis that excludes and transcends him" (NHNE 272, 274). Oates's own story concludes with a similar gesture: Matthew's wife, in the yard gardening responds to a call by opening *her arms for an embrace.*" (MI 378). Her "wordless, affirmation"—perhaps.

In her imitation of Henry James's "The Turn of the Screw," Oates actually tells two concurrent stories: one of a nephew, accompanying his dying uncle to a seaside resort, the second of an observer of this scene. Complete with a discussion about the existence of ghosts, the appearance of strange letters, a relationship that seems to exist between the nephew and the observer, the Oates version uniquely parallels its model. Focusing on the questions of what is real, what created, imagined, "made up," both stories explore the relatedness of art and life, of art and reality.

When she models a story on James Joyce's "The Dead," she is careful to capture the mood of the original—a party, the knowledge of a death, even the smallest detail of the snow. The snow falls in Joyce's work on both the living and the dead; Oates concludes with the snow "falling shapelessly upon them all" (MI 488)—the living, the lover. And the dead, the author. The sterility and vacuity of their lives is underscored in Oates by the almost frenzied exchange of partners. Husbands and lovers, wives and mistresses, relationships are begun and ended at whim. Ilena, the author, is virtually a living death, tottering on the brink of suicide by her pill-taking and drinking. She is more dead than alive. She is founder and member, as it were, of her fictional suicide club. Unable to affirm herself through lasting relationships, through her success as a writer, through her career as a teacher, she drifts without direction. The painful truth is anesthetized by liquor and drugs so that she does not have to feel the intense pain of being alive, of loving and giving, of caring. She is dead as a personality. The difference between Oates's and Joyce's stories is significant. There is an element of hope in Joyce; Gabriel has been quickened to new life by what he has learned and experienced. Ilena and Gordon lie together in her hotel bed; she swooning from the pills and alcohol, he tenderly caring for her, without any response. She thinks she is dying; perhaps she will not escape death this time. She feels she has drifted back to protoplasm, devoid of personality, a mere substance. Once again Oates has given a picture of death-in-life.

The city cannot redeem the human heart; in the city life is reduced to the "daily heart-breaking struggle over money, waged against every other ant-like inhabitant of the city."[46] Viewed from that perspective, urban life is not only alien to community but destructive of it. Man is not only isolated from his fellow man but also forced to fight against him for his daily bread. In the same context, Oates speaks of the "citizens of the demonic factory-world,"[47] a world which demands the "exorcism of 'evil' "[48] if man is ever to achieve affirmation.

The city teeming with unhappy, unfulfilled human beings is the ambiance of Oates's fiction. Yet social violence often only mirrors personal violence; the 1967 Detroit riots recounted in *them* merely reflect on a wider scale and scope the turbulent lives of the Wendall family. From the opening pages of the narrative, which depict the horror of Loretta's being awakened by a shot and the warm wetness of the blood of her lover in the bed beside her, to the convulsive

[18]

riots and senseless killings, the horrific pattern is repeated over and over again.

The cities of Oates's fiction range from the race track center at Cherry River, which is the setting for suicide and rioting, the migrant centers which spawn hatred and despair, the posh anonymous suburban locales breeding neuroses and murder, the metropolitan quagmire of inhumanities and injustice—the catalogue is complete. No urban setting escapes her critical and discerning eye. There is no relief and no getting away; not even constant moving about, as most of her characters do, can afford release.

Although the settings seem to change, the place names differ, the geographical locales are different, they are all the same. They are the "Unreal City" of the Wasteland which is nowhere and everywhere. They are Detroit, Chicago, Cedar Grove, Fernwood; they are north and south, large and small, urban and rural—but they are all the same. They are the savage jungle, the urban wilderness where the only rule of life is dog-eat-dog. There are no victors, there are only those who are not quite so badly hurt. There is rioting in Detroit and in Cherry River, but only the place names are different. There are migrant groups; there are the Wendalls, the Everetts, the Walpoles, but the names only are changed. If anomie and dislocation are the characteristics of the "nation of strangers," Oates effectively and tragically portrays that condition. The tragedy that befalls the Wendalls is repeated in the chronicle of the Everetts and the Walpoles. The cyclical nature of tragedy seems to deepen the sense of despair and futility.

From the Cherry River of *With Shuddering Fall* to the Grosse Pointe of *Do With Me What You Will*, the only change Oates's cities undergo is to become worse. Karen and Shar are destroyed by each other in Cherry River, and their tragedies could have taken place anywhere; Cherry River is not essential to their fates. In Oates's later fiction, the action is often more rooted in the setting. Karen and Shar's violent relationship does not need a city setting: they would or could destroy each other anywhere.

In a later work, *A Garden of Earthly Delights*, the location plays a more integral role in the drama. The lives of the Walpoles, who must move five times in eight chapters, are little by little eroded by each different setting. They are forced by the repeated moves to fight harder and more desperately for their existence. Relationships, strained at best, erupt into violent feuds, leading at one time to murder and at another to flight. The mobility of the migrants, which their very survival requires, is mirrored in the socially necessitated mobility of the Everetts, the expensive people. So much dislocation enforced by economic pressures takes its toll of the human beings. A sense of isolation, of futility and uprootedness forces people, as the novel so well describes, into artificial relationships. Community cannot be created without some sense of rootedness.

The city is not the only target of Oates's criticism of society. She is very much at home with an academic setting and has recently brought out an entire volume of short stories using the university as the principal locale. She is no more partial to the academic world than to any other familiar setting; the chilling inhumanity of academia she describes is not unlike the vivid accounts of unkindness and destructive relationships found elsewhere in her works. From Wanda Barnett, who gets taken in and betrayed by Saul Bird and his pseudo-revolutionary group, to Ron Blass, who is both exposed and exonerated as a plagiarist by his colleagues, Oates is cutting in her description of the brutality and competitiveness of the campus.

Here, as elsewhere, Oates employs borrowed ironic titles: "Up From Slavery" deals with a black professor who hires, then succeeds in having fired, a young white woman who is convinced blacks and women have been similarly discriminated against; in "Pilgrim's Progress" Wanda learns a difficult lesson in betrayal; "Birth of Tragedy" narrates the situation of an inexperienced teaching assistant who tells his students his theory of tragedy—and is dropped from the graduate program.

As Oates has been a teacher on university campuses, it is not surprising to read her condemnations of aspects of the academic world. What is surprising, however, is the seemingly autobiographical story, "Angst." Here Oates not only castigates elements of university life but also strikes out in self-mockery against the established and prestigious organizations, namely the MLA. Bernadine Donovan, a promising young author, is attending the MLA in Chicago where she is on a panel as well as the topic for discussion at another session.

A critic's comment during the seminar that Bernadine is "one of *the* finest of living American women writers, though she 'had not yet located her true subject or a style in which to express it' " (HG 191) is not unlike some of the criticism leveled against Oates's own fiction.

At the session devoted to Bernadine Donovan's own fiction, which the author herself attends registered as B. G. Sullivan, a paper compares her to Virginia Woolf. A second paper describes her fiction as having "real *messages*" antithetical to the obvious statements in the works; it argues that her "little novels" are "celebrations of nihilism . . . dark rejoicings over the fact that *civilization as we know it is finished*" and that she is *not writing* a "celebration of order and hope for redemption." The third paper is interrupted by a red-haired woman who claims to be Donovan and who suggests that Swift, rather than Woolf, was the model for one of her earlier works.

Knowing Oates's aversion for attention, her apparent disdain of critics makes it difficult to see Bernadine Donovan in any other light than as a persona of the author. One cannot but wonder if the misreading of Donovan's fiction is not a rebuttal to those critics who have failed to appreciate and understand Oates's own fiction.

Oates also employs the shopping center as metaphor of the impermanence of human relations and the vacuity of lives in several of her short pieces. In "Years of Wonder" and "Stalking" there is an especially poignant use of the mall. Both narratives deal with young girls, the emptiness of whose lives is reflected in their flight to the crowded and anonymous mall. Gretchen, believing she is being "stalked" by an Invisible Adversary, runs to the mall where she shoplifts and destroys clothes in her flight (MI 171–79). In "Years of Wonder," thirteen-year-old Doreen, spends a considerable part of her life escaping with her friends to a maze-like mall with twenty-eight identical doors, double thermopane, which open automatically to impersonal shops and anonymous shoppers (S 189). The very title, "Years of Wonder," is sadly ironic: a youthful, energetic teenager, the wonders of whose life are potted geraniums, a caged parrot at Newberry's, and an unkempt and untalented portrait artist. It is a world of fast-food chains and maze-like malls, of orphaned children with living, unconcerned parents.

A "given" of Oates's society is, as she writes in "Plot," "the deteriorating nature of human relationships in America today." It is a world where one person can say to another: "I hope that from now on we can be friends, and forget each other' " (MI 198, 70).

When Sarah, the teen-age narrator of "In the Warehouse," kills her companion by pushing her down the stairs, the scene is grotesquely described: "A dark stain explodes out from her and pushes the dust along before it, everything speeded up by her violent squirming." The grotesqueness of the physical description, however, is overshadowed by the emotional reality when, twenty years later, she recalls the incident with no remorse. "There is a great shadowy space about me, filled with waiting: waiting to cry, to feel sorry . . . I have never felt sorry" (G 79, 80).

It is a world where an adolescent can kill her friend and never feel guilt ("In the Warehouse"); where a father can walk out on his family with his wife's young relative, whom he has gotten pregnant, and then kill himself in an auto crash ("Ruth"). In Oates's fictional world marriages and infidelities are coordinates, crossing with a tragic predictability; it is a world of persons devoid of moral responsibility—to themselves and to others. The first of "Five Confessions" is "I can't be faithful to you, or anyone" (AS 11). Physical deaths and spilling of blood are only emblematic of the spiritual suicides and the psychological assassinations in this world.

Running throughout Oates's fiction is the persistent absence of community, of loving, supportive, enduring commitments to others. This lack is evidenced in marriages which end in divorce or separation, in familial ties which do not last, in friendships which terminate in betrayal. The failures of human commitments are not only caused by fickleness and lack of character but often they are motivated by malicious and sinister reasons. Franklin Ambrose in "Up From Slavery" turns against his protégé, Molly Holt, out of rage at her remarks regarding discrimination. He feels wronged and betrayed by her and seeks revenge by turning his colleagues in the

English Department against her. In the end, however, he is unaware of what it is he has really done; he accepts no responsibility—much less blame—for the situation and returns to his home and family, triumphant and a little melancholy, not out of remorse but out of self-pity.

In "The Stone House," Ken Thomas learns a difficult lesson in human behavior when he encounters a young fruit picker, Linda. Oates sets up the dynamic juxtaposition between Ken's schooled education, his wealth, and his stone house with Linda's worldly experience, her poverty, and her trailer. After Linda seduces the naïve Ken, he makes her a proposal of marriage—only to find, as he dresses, a man's dirty sock under the bed. But Ken's delusions are shattered: "It had seemed to him then that her soft confident body defined the rich limitations of what was real, just as it had seemed to him that this trailer, with its junk and sweetish-sour smell, would be a place of violent initiation, and not just another warmer, more confused, more bitterly deceptive place of imprisonment like his family's stone house" (G 249). In the end he leaves the trailer and returns to his stone house, feeling a sense of suffocation and of shame. Linda, on the other hand, has had a pleasant day with him, her fun in the bed, and successfully conned him out of fifty dollars —to make up for what she could have made picking fruit.

Even stranger dynamics and games are played by Gerald and Andrea in "The Imposters." They had at one time been married to each other and are separated, when they meet unexpectedly in Provincetown. Introduced to each other as if they were strangers, they pretend not to know each other and engage in the customary small talk of people newly met—where are you from, what do you do. Later during a party they go off to the beach together and shed their imposter masks; they resume their relationship with one another. Lying in bed with Andrea, Gerald thinks "Time had been blocked out and now there was no secret between them, they were free, they were back at the beginning. Nothing had been lost, not yet. Everything was ahead of them. Andrea was asleep or he would have explained it to her" (G 187–88). One is left wondering which mask, which pretense is the more horrific—the pretense of not acknowledging each other or that of believing everything was ahead of them.

Linguistic sleight-of-hand almost destroys the young woman in "I Must Have You." The smooth rhetoric of her psychiatrist-lover deceives her, making the reality of his departure even harder for her to accept. Having told her " 'Bonds are made between people that extend beyond their physical existences....We don't have to live together permanently to love ... to be united in love ... No bond of love is ever broken ... People leave one another. People die. But the bonds between them are real' " (G 177). When he is finished with her and ready to move on, these words are expected to assuage her pain. Nothing lasts, nothing is permanent.

Oates artistically weaves into her stories her thematic concern for communication by references to mail: the location of a mail box is often as important as the location of a home; messages of life and death and reunion are announced through the mail. Some communications, however, fail—some are not received, some unopened. Her story, "Explorations," deals with marital infidelity and an incompleted communication. Sometime after Fritz Risner leaves Margaret and her husband, when he and Margaret have had an affair, he dies as a suspected suicide. Margaret and her husband are shocked by the news. Later a letter to Margaret arrives from Risner, having been missent and forwarded several times, but she chooses not to open it, she destroys it. Whatever Risner had intended to say to her is forever lost.

When the most basic cohesive bonds, that between a man and woman, between a parent and child, a brother and sister, are so mutable, there is little hope of creating community. The mainspring of tragedy in Oates's works is not that the city destroys community but that human beings fail to create it. The single most significant factor in the failure to establish community is the person, the person who selfishly destroys another. Sociologists are quick to point out that only in an experience of community is the self ever fully experienced. The "we" of community is prior to the "I" of self-identity. In Oates's fictive world, there are no available communities, hence no fully actualized personalities. A destructive chain of events is thus set up: the person lacking self-identity seeks community; not finding it, he is thrown deeper into his vacuum. Without a secure sense of self, he cannot enter into a relationship with another—not even the community of marriage. In all of Oates, there is no marriage that achieves the fulfillment of its partners. In fact, marriages and affairs are as casually entered into and broken off as one would arrange a hair appointment. The impermanence of human relationships attests to Oates's sense that "nothing lasts."

The absence of any functioning community in her fiction points up the tremendous need for such in the fictive society of her works and in the lives of her characters. Nowhere are there cohesive bonds—not in family relationships, in friendship, in the work community, in the neighborhood, or the gang, in male-female ties—in the whole of her fiction, there is no enduring bond among human beings. And, by this very omission, she unequivocally underlines the need for community.

Using the term "love" rather casually, Oates defines two kinds of love: one which creates the other person and one which destroys. Her fiction deals mainly with the latter: "a bizarre mysterious, anti-social" emotion which instead of being life-giving is really "murderous."[49] There can be no hope of establishing community based on this second type of "love."

Joyce Carol Oates's women are stereotypical portraits of frustrated, neurotic human beings psychically crippled by the events of their lives and the tragic frustrations with which they cannot cope. Their only redeeming quality is that they do survive, they manage to make it through these all but overwhelming circumstances. Only about Loretta Wendall of *them* is there something admirable. She, unlike most of Oates's women characters, cannot be broken—not by the murder of her lover beside her in bed, not by her rape by the policeman investigating the murder, not by her children, not by the urban riots—nothing destroys Loretta as the other women, Clara, Karen, Nada are destroyed. Her achievement is not only that she survives, but that she also grows stronger and tougher through the experience.

In much of Oates's early fiction women survive by having nervous breakdowns as Karen Herz and Clara Revere do. But by the time she writes *Do With Me What You Will*, her female characters have matured and are more capable of enduring the hardships of life. Elena Howe, heroine of the most recent novel, leaves her husband, Marvin, to join her lover, Jack Morrissey. This final act of the novel raises the extremely ambiguous question: is it assertion or capitulation? Nevertheless, Elena is able to act; she is not passively victimized as most of her fictive ancestors are. Critics, however, are sharply divided on the issue of the success or failure of *Do With Me What You Will*. Christopher Lehmann-Haupt defends the book as Oates's response to the women's liberation movement.[50] Mary Ellmann labels the author a "hortatory feminist" and declares that the "lesson" of the novel is "not Love Conquers All, but Women Must Assert Themselves."[51] Regardless of the critical achievement of the novel, Oates is in this novel creating a new type of female character. This creation may be a long way from Nora Helman of Henrik Ibsen's *A Doll's House* to whom Elena is frequently likened, but she is radically different from the anemic, listless, passive characters of Oates's earlier fiction. The gradual evolution is traceable in her works.

In a continuing pattern, the women of Oates's short fiction are despairing, unfulfilled, and frustrated. They are victims of rape, of sexual fantasies, of masochistic relationships—struggling, nevertheless, "to create a fixed universe" (G 129), to discover or affirm a sense of order or direction from the shambles in which they find their lives. They seek a sense of wonder, they need a new consciousness.

True to the pattern of their fictional antecedents, the women in *The Goddess and Other Women* are victims of male domination, of hysteria and breakdowns, and the typical coping behavior of an Oates heroine continues to be having a mental breakdown. Without the power to assert themselves, her women crumble. Fragile personalities shatter; only the strong survive.

The Goddess of this collection, as critics have noted, is Kali, the Hindu goddess of destruction and death, the antithesis of a principle of creation. Kali is the prototype of a number of Oates women, and particularly of the women in this volume. In "Concerning the Case of Bobby T.," Frances, a young white girl, accuses Bobby T. of attacking her although she was responsible for what happened. As a result of her lying, Bobby T. spends the next nineteen years in jails and mental hospitals. When finally released, the once fun-loving, good-looking black youth is practically a vegetable, afraid of people, panicked by the sight of traffic, unable to do anything for himself, destroyed by Frances.

Another teen-age girl, Ruth, is responsible for destroying not only a person, but a whole family. After Ruth comes to live with the Wreszin family, she and Mr. Wreszin fall in love. She tells Wreszin she's pregnant, and as they are running away together, he crashes the car and kills himself as all the while Ruth protests " 'Why—why —it isn't my fault—' " (G 104–5). Elsewhere in the volume, a younger version of the Kali-women appears in "Blindfold" in the person of Betsy, a child who is jubilant over the death of her uncle, who she fantasizes has molested her.

The motif of the destructive woman is repeated over and over in the collection; she is Katherine, the compassionless social worker; she is the *magna mater* obsessed with achieving order at any cost; she is Nancy, who sets off small avalanches down a hillside on a man who had been walking with her. When she is not destroying others, she is destroying herself or succumbing to the pressures of daily life. One out of every four of Oates's women requires some kind of psychiatric care. Some are suicidal, some have never grown up, despite their ages, and are looking for fathers rather than husbands. What finally is disconcerting about Oates's women is that they are weak, spiritually impoverished, devoid of beauty, morally bankrupt—in a word, unfeminine.

When Oates focuses on the "love" between a man and a woman, she more often than not calls attention to the destructive element. In her poem, "Anonymous Sins," the title poem of one of her volumes, the female speaker says, "I gaze down upon / a mangled body / seeing my love / is endless." As a result of this she comes to "understand how / a woman is used / used up / how a man moves / too abrupt at any pace" (AS 73–74). Love mangles her body and so uses her up. Another poem "To Whose Country Have I Come?" from the same volume also speaks of this mangling: "*We are born only to be broken / in one single lavishing / of love*" (AS 56).

Elsewhere she bitterly identifies women with blood—menstruation, abortion: "we are bloodstained women growing fiercely / up out of girls," "stained with splashes / of old food and old love," "we belong to men and answer to their last names" (AF 14). Used and abused, denied identity and fulfillment, Oates's women too often supinely accept the statement "we are born only to be broken." And break they do.

Oates is not a feminist writer; in fact, she appears impervious to feminist concerns and to the cause of women's liberation. One explanation for this may lie in her failure to project any prophetic vision in her fiction. Oates appears to be concerned with describing human life as it is—not as it might be. Life, as gleaned from her fiction, is cruel, destroying, purposeless, and unless one realizes this, he will probably be swept into the vortex. The only way out of this death-in-life is through an awareness of the human condition by which one may seize the remnants of his life and reshape them into something meaningful and whole. And this is a human problem not a feminist problem.

Oates does not stand in extraordinarily high repute with feminist critics largely because her fiction lacks strong, self-determining, fulfilled women. Instead, it tends to focus on weak women, women whose lives have failed, often because of extreme dependence on male strength. The heroine of "I Must Have You" is a typical Oates female; she depends entirely on a male for the meaning of her life. At the conclusion of the narrative, she has been abandoned by her lover and begins to despair, but she knows she is saved when she hears a man's voice on the phone. "A voice in my ear was asking me to repeat; to go slowly. It was a man's voice, so my panic went down. A man's voice .... It was a man's voice and so I knew I would be saved, I knew I would be loved; I obeyed it and began to speak more slowly" (G 181). She, not unlike most of Oates's women characters, lives to be loved, pampered, and supported by a man. In this case the man from whom she seeks all this is a psychiatrist playboy who, walking out on her, explains, "I can't give birth to you" (G 180). Although he severs the parasitic relationship, one wonders who had the greater need. He, however, can coolly walk away to his next affair while she succumbs to despair—a typical Oates heroine.

In the whole fictional world Oates has created, there is not one convincingly fulfilled or happy woman. Many of her women are, in fact, the antithesis of the liberated woman. They are cunning, jealous, suicidal, petty, fawning, miserable women who want comfort, sex, money, and men. It is, perhaps, by the absence of any truly feminine and fulfilled women that Oates best speaks for the "cause." As she strongly cries for the need of community through a body of writings devoid of loving, communal ties, so she points to the need for mature, self-determining women through their nonexistence in her fiction.

Oates will never be a Doris Lessing much less an Erica Jong. Nor will she be a supporter of women's rights through hortatory rhetoric—even in fictional form. But she will and she does subtly bring before her readers a picture of the pitiable lives of unliberated women. For Oates there could be no more powerful way to speak to the need than by focusing on its absence.

If her female characters are victimized and more often than not nonassertive and powerless, it is to children that the author looks as a source of hope, as a potentiality of society to change. In discussing *The Dollmaker*, Oates laments the fact of the children's enthusiastic acquiescence to capitalistic values, calling it one of the "most depressing aspects of the novel."[52] The two avenues to salvation for Harriette Arnow—and by implication for Joyce Carol Oates as well—are love and art. Love, particularly the unsullied and unpretentious love of children, love not contaminated by worldly values and the pursuit of purely economic gains. Tragically, children quickly learn they must sell themselves to survive. If Arnow's novel succeeds in narrating the horrific account of children selling themselves, much of Oates's work reveals the same disdainful tragedy. The children of Oates's own novels are equally depressing.

They are murderers, victims of kidnappings and rapes and suicides. Yet through children the shallowness of the lives of the adults and the hatreds, fierce or petty, become apparent. As one critic notes, it is only a child who can see hatred in *Expensive People* and, sadly, it is the child who suffers most as the result.

The Wreszin children, like so many of Oates's young characters, are "already overburdened with other memories . . . They had been brought up to think of their lives as taking place in a kind of puddle that was always getting smaller . . . they knew somehow that the puddle was shrinking and they might someday drown in air they weren't ready for . . . . They are not children, they are miniature adults" (G 86) laden with the weariness of life, without hope and without joy.

In another sense, Oates's children are identified as "disguised adults" (G 58). They have no childhood, no youth. Philip, Saul Bird's son, is described as "dwarfish, rather than small, wise and almost wooden" (HG 47). He is not a boy, he is a wooden miniature of the male adult.

In the same review of *The Dollmaker*, Oates writes movingly of the awful human tragedy replicated in the lives of children. "The fear of anarchy, shared by all of us who have been children, materializes in the constant struggle of children to maintain their identities, striking and recoiling from one another: in miniature they live out tragic scenarios, the pressure upon the human soul in our age, the overcrowding of life, the suffocating of the personality under the weight of sheer numbers, noise, confusion."[53] While she places on children the hope of changing society, she resignedly observes and recounts their destruction by the society they are potentially capable of changing. The children of her fiction are the tragic victims of the diminished urban world.

TWO

A vision of violence

Where love stops, power begins, and violence, and terror.

Carl Gustav Jung, *The Undiscovered Self*

Joyce Carol Oates's fictive world is violent, replete with nightmare, destruction, and futility, with a catalogue of horrors as incredibly real as the front pages of a metropolitan daily. Any understanding of her fiction is contingent upon an understanding of the place violence has in her tragic vision. For Oates, life, conceived in terms of a brutal struggle for survival against the world and against one's fellow human beings, can only be conquered through violence. The one recourse man has to achieve a sense of self-affirmation in the "cheap, flashy wasteland of modern America"[1] is violence. Often his only avenue to a sense of integrity and selfhood is that of violence.

In the introduction to her collection of essays on the tragic forms of literature, *The Edge of Impossibility*, Oates explains in part the reason for the centrality of violence in her fictive world and in her thought. Denying modern nihilism, she questions how this assumption accounts "for its very shape [which is] the structural consummation of violent action?" Based on fear, art, she maintains, is "built around violence, around death" (EOI 6). Even fictional characters who seem incapable of performing violent acts themselves participate in violence by being victims. From violence, in Oates's world, there is no escaping.

Continuously, her fiction searches out and exposes the very root of violence: a sense of personal impotence. At the heart of violence in her world is the absolute and utter inability to affirm oneself—without which the person is unable to live fully as a human being, to define, affirm, and assert himself, and to enter satisfying relationships with other persons.

1

In his recent study *Power and Innocence: A Search for the Sources of Violence*, psychologist Rollo May confirms from his vantage point of psychotherapy what Oates states in her fiction. May isolates three components of violence: a need for meaning or significance; a desire for ecstasy or fascination; and an impulse to gainsay one's whole being, to risk all. One or more of these drives propel a man to violence. May repeatedly stresses his conviction that violence arises from powerlessness; when the human person experiences only his own inability to assert or define himself, he resorts to violence as a means to overcome this impotence. This is true of man individually and collectively, according to May. Personal feelings of powerlessness lead to individual acts of violence, and racial or group feelings lead to rioting and revolution. The reason for this, the psychologist maintains, is that impotence corrodes self-esteem.[2] For the individual or the group to achieve any victory over feelings of inadequacy and powerlessness, the one available means is violence.

In *The Face of Violence: An Essay with a Play*, Jacob Bronowski further enunciates the basic assumption of Rollo May that violence is caused by a sense of powerlessness. In a passage that touches not only on the cause of violence but also on its object, Bronowski asserts that "at the heart of our violence, in act or in feeling, lies our wish to show ourselves men of will. Since society is an instrument for controlling our chaotic wills, the gesture of violence we make is anti-social; we invent a symbol for the forces of society, obscure and impersonal, which shall be our scapegoat. But the symbol is only a mask for the fear of each of us that society thwarts what is best and personal in him. We fear that society disregards us. In the wilderness of the cities, we look for respect." He concludes that violence "is an impulse we all share. The love of violence is ... the ancient and symbolic gesture of man against the constraints of society."[3]

When Oates translates these theoretical statements into fictional ones, the horrifying truth becomes readily available. The love of violence and its fascination and ecstasy are recurrent themes in her works. The sense of personal powerlessness drives men like Shar Rule, Howard Wendall, Brock Botsford, and Jules Wendall to lash out against societal constraints, to kill, to inflict injury on others; it drives women like Karen Herz, Clara Walpole, and Elena Howe to destroy others, their lovers, their children, their husbands. Oates's characters are unconsciously drawn to violence, "itchy" for something to happen, easily provoked to violent deeds.

Part of this attraction of violence, as Hannah Arendt explains, is the speed with which it can overcome its immediate provocation. "To resort to violence when confronted with outrageous events or conditions," she writes, "is enormously tempting because of its inherent immediacy and swiftness."[4] Not only as a means of destroying one's adversary, violence or destructiveness may also spring from an effort to "transcend the triviality of [human] life ... to seek adventure, to look beyond and even to cross the limiting frontier of human existence," according to Erich Fromm.[5] This desire to overcome the trivial is likewise triggered by the feeling of impotence, a frustration with life.

Arendt draws a sharp distinction between power and violence, asserting that while their interrelatedness cannot be denied, the fundamental differences must be preserved. She defines power as the human ability to act in concert: power belongs to a group—as opposed to strength, which, she maintains, is singular and individual. Violence is distinguished from both power and strength by virtue of its nature as instrument. Moreover, the affinity between violence and strength is derived from the fact that violence is used to multiply strength until it becomes a substitute for it. "Violence can always destroy power . . . What never can grow out of it is power."[6] The delusion that violence always confers power frequently confounds the attempts of those who resort to violence to achieve anything permanent. How well Arendt's theory articulates the distinction between power and violence may be tested against Oates's fictional depictions of the two entities. There are ample demonstrations of the inefficacy of violence to achieve long-lasting results. A violent deed, a murder, a riot does not exorcise, as the doer hopes, the powerlessness which initially prompted the violence.

Saul Bird perhaps best articulates the drive toward violence experienced by Oates's characters. Explaining his radical position to a new faculty member, Saul notes, " 'Intelligent discourse between humanists is the only means of bringing about a revolution—until the need for violence is more obvious, I mean.' " Later when specific plans are being laid for demonstrations, two rhetorical questions are raised: "How can one live in such a rotten society? Why not destroy it with violence?" (HG 44, 50). Many of Oates's characters are convinced they cannot live in the chaos and confusion of society and turn to violence to assert themselves and destroy that society.

Ken Thomas, humiliated in his fleeting encounter with the fruit-picker, Linda, is drawn to violence by the satisfaction he feels it would bring him, "the beatific gratification one might gladly sacrifice one's life for, discarding it angrily, without thought" (S 248). But his violence has no direction; he cannot identify what he would like to destroy so he remains hurt, beaten, and inert. Unlike Mott, who lashes out against his caseworker, Thomas has nothing to aim at.

But the question of whether or not violence can help to create the self is seriously debated among sociologists, philosophers, and psychologists. Jean-Paul Sartre maintains in his highly controversial introduction to Frantz Fanon's *The Wretched of the Earth* that

[34]

"this irrepressible violence is neither sound and fury, nor the resurrection of savage instincts, nor even the effect of resentment: it is man re-creating himself."[7]

This twofold aspect of violence, the ability to destroy the "enemy" and the ability to transcend the trivial, Joyce Carol Oates continually explores in her writings. Throughout her works, however, she insists on the ability of violence to help the individual achieve a sense of identity and wholeness. In assigning to violence this function she is not far from Flannery O'Connor, whom she praises for this very emphasis.[8] The effort to achieve personal integrity is begun through violence insofar as the person in this manner asserts and defines himself as unique and other. A fundamental difference, however, exists between the use of violence by the two authors: in O'Connor's works violence has redemptive value, the character who suffers violence is changed, regenerated by the experience. In Oates's world, violence is performed by the character himself, motivated by his own sense of powerlessness. It does not radically change his life, although it may be a means of his temporarily transcending his petty existence. There is an unchangeability about the lives of Oates's characters. No form, no amount of violence brings about a new consciousness in her characters, as happens in O'Connor.

Oates's fiction is filled with violence because the society it describes is likewise filled with violence. Her writings presuppose a nightmare world which challenges the very limits of man's endurance and tries his spirit to the breaking point. Violence can bring man to the brink of self-discovery and often serves as an affirmation of his humanity. But ultimately, it has no lasting effect; violence cannot confer power, which is what those who turn to violence seek. It may for a time assuage one's feelings of impotence, but it does not permanently change his life.

While O'Connor may be eloquent as a stylist, Joyce Carol Oates argues, she is also a "primitive": "she insists that only through an initiation by violence does man 'see.' "[9] This "seeing" is the beginning of self-discovery which in Oates, as well as O'Connor, is the absolute prerequisite of self-fulfillment. Violence becomes the agency of self-discovery and self-assertion. The basic difference, how-

[35]

ever, remains: in O'Connor's fiction, the characters achieve regeneration through violence, and in Oates's they are only destroyed, they cannot take the final step to self-fulfillment.

A character may also be drawn to violence in Oates's world by the sheer excitement of a violent act. The intrigue of or attraction to violence may be the ecstasy which follows the successful rebellion or deed of violence. When May describes this component of violence, he supports his theory by citing various studies of the effects of war on the human psyche; he concludes that violence generates an experience of ecstasy. In a much earlier study of the moral effects and equivalents of war, William James wrote that it is the very horrors of war which create its fascination.[10] Recent studies of war have verified this thesis.

Integrally related to ecstasy is the element of risk; in violence one often risks all for this end. There is also in the ecstasy which comes from violence a "lust for destruction," further identified as an "atavistic urge" to kill and smash things. May identifies this as "a joy in violence that takes the individual out of himself and pushes him toward something deeper and more powerful than he has previously experienced." May also enunciates an interesting corollary to the relationship between violence and creativity when he observes that as long as the artist can create, he does not have to resort to violence, because the drive to create in art is the same as the drive to violence.[11] Once again the twofold nature of violence comes under scrutiny: creative-destructive, liberating-enslaving.

There is yet another way in which violence is related to wholeness. The human must be related to other persons, and the denial or frustration of this necessity is a short road to crime and violence. A fleeting sense of brotherhood often results from the pursuit of violence, the transient fraternity of people working together for a common purpose. When one's entire environment militates against establishing meaningful human relationships, the natural tendency, in Oates's world, is to lash out against that milieu. Anaïs Nin explains this connection between the failure or inability to achieve satisfying relationships and the violent crime: "The impotence to relate to another is the impotence to love others and from this impotence to crime is a natural step. . . . A frustrated need for intimacy may explode into crime." Today's fiction is obsessed with the violent, she laments, because violence has become a substitute for authentic self-affirmation. As a symptom of modern schizophrenia, violence becomes a means of asserting oneself, of triumphing over personal impotence. Violence, she continues, is used "in order to feel alive because the divided self feels its own death and seeks sensation to affirm its existence."[12] Thus violence is either a means of achieving or a surrogate for self-affirmation in the post-absurdist world. Similarly, Iris Murdoch protests against so much violence in modern fiction while simultaneously conceding its unquestionable role in human life.[13]

Repeatedly in her stories and novels, Oates traces the tragic connection between the failure to establish meaningful human relations and the recourse to violence, often to murder. In *Wonderland*, Jesse Harte kills his wife and family and himself because he cannot relate to them as husband and father. Later his only surviving son, Jesse, is nearly killed by Trick Monk because the latter cannot enter into or sustain a normal, healthy human relationship. Jesse's smothering love for his daughter, Shelley, all but drives her to kill herself as the cycle is repeated: the absence or impotence of love essential for a sense of wholeness drives the character to express and assert himself through violence.

In *Do With Me What You Will*, Rachel accuses Jack Morrissey of being a " 'bullying bastard.' " Moved by anger and shame at Jack's attempt to force a black minister to let him stir up a case involving the shooting death of a young black youth by a state trooper, she accuses him of using his power to try to manipulate the man. " 'You —you come out to their house—you sit there—You use your mouth the way other men use their fists or knives or—You bastard! Bastard! I know what it's like to lie down flat on my back and to have a bastard like you stick himself in me, like it was a knife or a gun or— prodding, stabbing, sticking—And a bastard like you, because he's on top, he gives all the commands—*lie still, turn over, get on your knees, put your face down in the dirt*—and the niggers and anybody else on the bottom had better move fast—' " (DWM 246). Impassionedly, vividly, she describes in the metaphor of making love the violence heaped on those "on the bottom."

All her writing is about human relationships, Oates insists.[14] Yet paradoxically no one in her whole fictive, almost Balzacian world can achieve satisfying or fulfilling relationships. The failure of parents to love their children produces such grotesques as the offspring of Dr. Pederson, the obese child-murderer Richard Everett, the vagrant Clara Walpole, the vapid Elena Howe. The infidelity of wife and husband or lovers is another recurrent theme. And although there is no way in which love is a glib or facile solution to the problems of the human predicament, its quintessential role in human fulfillment is irrevocably established in her writing. Failure to love leaves her characters with no recourse except violence.

Violence is also part of man's efforts to exercise some control over his world. " 'To be safe from violence you have to be violent yourself,' "—Lowry explains to Clara (GED 149). One is violent first, before he becomes the victim. Violence is an escape from passivity; even if one is destroyed in the end, it is better to have taken the first step of being violent oneself. Martin Heidegger in his *Introduction to Metaphysics* elaborates on this principle. Violence is the direct result of violated being, he philosophizes. "Man is the violent one. . . . He uses power against the overpowering."[15]

The characters of Oates's world try desperately to control the events and situations which tend to destroy or lessen their sense of self. The gnawing bitterness of Carleton Walpole, forced to move every few months up and down and across the United States in search of work and food, is the direct result of his life situation. The ultimate humiliation comes, ironically after Carleton has already killed a man, and finds in a migrant camp in New Jersey that the number on his shack has been painted backwards. "Carleton stared at this figure in disgust, to think that he would have to live in a shanty with a six painted backwards on it, as if he himself had been stupid enough to do that" (GED 56). Beaten down, humiliated beyond his endurance, a man on the bottom, he turns to violence to assert himself and to drink to forget.

In his forensic study, *Violent Men*, Hans Toch provides a typology of violence useful in a consideration of the role of violence in the works of Joyce Carol Oates.[16] He divides his findings into two major categories based on the individual's conceptions of himself. In the first classification are those deeds of violence which are prompted by some motive of ego-preservation. Toch identifies six, labeling them: "rep defending," "norm enforcing," "self-image compensating" (further divided into self-image defending and self-image promoting), "self-defending," and "pressure removing." Violence motivated by one or more of these causes is largely for the purpose of enhancing one's image before oneself and others. The four subdivisions of the second grouping describe violent acts performed by an individual who regards himself and others as objects. In these cases the violence is directed toward another as thing not as a person. When he amplifies this typology, Toch explains that in "rep defending" the individual is driven to violence by his public image, which at all costs he must preserve and defend as in the case of Carleton's murder of Rafe. When violence is motivated by some undeclared rules, the individual acts out of a self-assigned mission and a world view in which violence is the norm, as in the riots in Cherry River and Detroit. Seeing others as potential physical dangers may prompt a man to violence; being unable to cope with pressures without exploding has the same effect. Many of Oates's characters are impulsively driven to violence, too, by their own inability to accept the vicissitudes of life. Two compensatory drives link violent acts with low self-esteem: in the first, the individual retaliates against those who confirm his low opinion of himself, and in the second, he seeks to prove his worth through violence. Obviously Rollo May's basic theory of impotence as the primary source of violence underpins the self-image compensating categories.

Bullying as a type of violence occurs when one individual overpowers others vulnerable to his force and strength; Jack Morrissey's bullying of the Reverend Efron exemplifies this category. When manipulation meets with resistance, the person inclined toward exploiting others may resort to violence. Likewise the self-indulging individual relies on violence when his own gratification is not served by others. The final category identifies violence as a result of internal pressures, modes, or feelings. As with any classification, the divisions seem to overlap at times, but the fundamental distinctions Toch insists upon serve to clarify the varied motives and occasions of violence.

Generally, Oates's violent characters belong to the self-image compensating category, as in the depictions of Swan Revere, Elena Howe, and Clara Walpole. But she does not by any means limit herself to this type of character. She is concerned with violence in human life as it springs from powerlessness and when it is turned outward against either another person or against society. Relentlessly, she searches out the causes. Her one hope for deliverance and redemption from the atrocities brought on by violence lies in children who have not learned violence as a way of life. In order to preserve this hope, Oates has no real children in her fictive world; all her young creations are miniature adults. When Clara runs away with Lowry who is older than she, he is apprehensive about her age and asks her, " 'How the hell old are you?' " To her response of eighteen, he says, " 'No, you're just a child.' " "'That word was one that had nothing to do with her—she exhaled her waiting breath in a sound of contempt. 'I'm not a—child,' she said angrily. 'I'm not a child, I never was.' " Her own boy Swan, encountering a child in a doctor's office, "could not remember ever having been a child" (GED 107, 423). From the first, Clara had recognized everything hard and strong in Lowry—present but diminished in the baby Swan. He, too, was a middle-aged child.

Nor is there a childhood for the Wendall children. Forced when very young to cope with the problems of adult life, the Wendalls learn the ways of aggression and self-preservation early. When he is not more than twelve or thirteen, Jules wonders if he had "ever been a child? Really a child? In the sense in which other people have been children? And what did it mean, to have been a child?" (them 97). Nothing in his experience can answer these questions; he had, in fact, never been a child and he had never known any other children.

Although Richard Everett lays claims to being a child, he really is not. If he ever was, it had not been for very long, as he recognizes when he writes his memoirs. "It was in Fernwood that I began to disintegrate as a child. You people who have survived childhood don't remember any longer what it was like. You think children are whole, uncomplicated creatures, and if you split them in two with a handy ax there would be all one substance inside, hard candy. But it isn't hard candy so much as a hopeless seething lava of all kinds, of things, a turmoil, a mess. And once the child starts thinking about this mess he begins to disintegrate as a child and turns into something else—an adult, an animal" (EP 32).

Robbed of childhood, forced into adult ways, Oates's characters learn that violence is a way of life: it is the only way some of them can survive. To escape from violence one must be the aggressor—a realization which beleaguers and ultimately destroys most of her characters.

2

With Shuddering Fall, Joyce Carol Oates's first novel, outlines the contours of her later works. Carefully etched in Shar Rule is a portrait of a "man of violence," (WSF 168) an impotent, pathetic racer who, frightened and threatened by the infatuation and the stirring of adolescent love of a young girl, destroys himself rather than open himself to a relationship of love and tenderness. A man with no sense of self, Shar must always prove and defend his self-image. To him love means the surrender of freedom, a price he cannot pay. Shar is the paradigm of many of Oates's later characters; while these achievements are less verbalized, less obvious than *With Shuddering Fall,* they nevertheless reverberate on the same note of violence and impotence. The themes of this first novel also recur with horrific persistence in her works. She is keenly aware of the sources of violence, both personal and collective, which she defines and articulates. Lured by the pseudosense of power and the ecstasy that accompanies violence, her characters resort to destruction and acts of violence in desperate attempts to assert and affirm themselves.

Oates sharply focuses on the sense of powerlessness and personal inadequacy that drives and propels a man to violence. Shar is incapable of loving and being loved, of asserting himself, of affirming himself. Once he fully realizes that Karen loves him—when she follows him to Cherry River—he cannot live with the realization and embarks on a deliberate course of self-destruction. Ultimately he is incapable of taking off his defensive mask of power.

Shar is often described as itching for violence, with a desire so great that his actions and reactions are reduced to an animal level. Looking at him one time, Karen reflects that his appearance suggests the "uneasiness of the predatory beast that suspects he can never achieve satiation" (WSF 166). He is threatened by tenderness; his power is challenged by human love, and since he has not learned that love itself is a kind of power, the first course open to him is flight. He must run from Karen, his "initial failure to escape her had decided everything" (WSF 172). He can neither deny nor accept her love. Having run once, only to find that she had followed him, having done everything conceivable to hurt her, only to discover her clinging to him, he drives his car into a wall and completes the conflagration dreamed of as a boy, begun when he burned his father in the cabin and concluded in his own fiery death.

Rather than creating him, renewing and supporting him, Karen's love poses an insurmountable threat to his precarious strength. He cannot accept her love and tries first to reject her; when this fails, rather than return her love, he destroys himself. Out of a sense of his deep personal powerlessness, masked by his pose of virility and physical prowess, he boasts of his pseudopower and his ability to make his own luck.

He sneers at the crowds who come, admiringly, to watch him race. He spurns Karen's youthful love, which, years before the violent episodes of the novel, he had caught a glimpse of. Her soul, he remembers, "had peered out at him dimpled, sly, it had calculated the distance between them—it had conquered him" (WSF 245). He then makes love to her so violently that it brings on an abortion, although he had not known she was pregnant. He prides himself on his facade of self-control, "his lack of emotions, his failure to involve himself seriously with anyone, his refusal to accept anything as permanent." But Karen's love has the power to unmask and ruin him. She shatters his cool composure, and her entry into his life marks the return of his "old desire for destruction." As delusion is heaped on delusion, Shar believes the "insane fragment of his life would be made whole—cleansed through violence, a communion of pain" (WSF 246).

Karen is not the innocent victim of this relationship, however. She is ruthless, coldly determined to win, to defeat Shar. When she realizes that he is weakening, giving up the game as she calls his pose of self-reliance, she refuses to stop playing herself. Accustomed as she had become "to a life that began nowhere and headed nowhere, geographically and morally [she] understood that she must not abandon the game herself but must continue to play it in secret, plotting and calculating her moves until victory was hers" (WSF 169). But the only way she can conquer Shar is through his death. Rather than create, her love destroys. Shar comes to realize this once when he violently makes love to her. "They had moved through their months together in an elaborate dance, always avoiding each other, at the same time luring and entrapping each other, and it was with disgust that Shar realized this mockery of love had not yet come to an end. He had not yet violated Karen's secrecy; she had eluded him. The communion of pain to which he had forced her brutally had given Shar to her but it had not given Karen to Shar" (WSF 247).

Karen's realization of her role in Shar's death is halting. In the streets of Cherry River, she can scream, " 'We are all killers' " (WSF 285); later she sees only Shar and her father as killers, losing all sight of her part in what has happened to both men. During a mass, after her release from the state hospital, she finally recognizes her power and her complicity. She can admit her initiation into the "communion of killers" and question whether the "skill of murder [has] to be learned" (WSF 312). In the end, Karen can begin to see that her playing the game with a hopelessly powerless man has caused his death. The recognition is achieved through violence.

In this first novel, Oates is careful to create an atmosphere

[43]

teeming with violence. Not only are her central characters, Karen and Shar, driven to violent acts—the major episodes revolve around fighting, rioting, suicide, abortion, rape—but also the whole world of the novel is violent. The potentially pastoral setting of Eden County is undercut from the opening description of the woods and streams. To Karen, the creek, which had been frozen over until recently, is "luring and sinister, and the rapids gurgled as if they gloated over its own violent metamorphosis" (WSF 17); the sun is "sullen." The physical world, as it were, mirrors the chaos and disorder of human life. Karen recalls the winter months when during the "worst days the snow looked like an incredible sifting of earth and heaven, blotting out both earth and heaven, reducing them to an insane struggle of white that struck at human faces like knifes. Summers reeked with heat, and heaven pressed downward so that the sun had to glare through skies of dust. Sometimes there would be holocausts of fire in the woods, churnings and twistings of white smoke rising into the white sky. The brutality of the land somehow evoked joy in Karen" (WSF 35).

But nature's violence is not willful as man's often is. Even that most potentially sacred and peaceful domain of human relationships, the family, is fraught with violence, anger, and hatred. There can be little question of the existence of love between Karen and her family, yet it is marred by hostility; the novel begins and ends with tense, angry scenes between Karen and her father. At the opening he forces her to accompany him to the squalid cabin of Rule and he is cruelly distant from her at the end—until he speaks, somewhat uncharacteristically, words of reconciliation to her after church. The intensity is never softened, the hurt never healed, the love never gentle or creative.

Fear, which may be directed toward something specific or may simply be nonspecified, naturally accompanies violence. Shar specifically fears Karen and the entrapment of her love, and they both have an awesome fear of Max. But a more poignant fear is expressed by the storekeeper from whom they seek shelter at the beginning of their flight. He expresses to Shar his vague and uneasy fear about what the young boy they see outside the store might do—because the youth is hungry.

Oates's choice of Nietzsche's "What is done out of love always takes place beyond good and evil" as an epigraph to the novel does not elucidate her thematic concern with violence and its sources; it only generates more ambiguity. The characters in this fictive world do not act out of love but out of impotence and a lack of self-worth. Driven to violence in an effort to recover a sense of their self-image or to assert themselves, these powerless people do not operate out of love. Consequently their acts may not be judged beyond good or evil; there are strong moral implications in everything they do. The epigraph, therefore, which implies approbation of any deed performed out of love serves more to obfuscate than to clarify the ethical dimensions which Joyce Carol Oates seems concerned to preserve.

In her trilogy on the three classes of society, Joyce Carol Oates demonstrates that no stratum of society is immune from violence. The brutal, physical violence of the migrants is transmogrified into the muted but nonetheless destructive, psychological violence of the expensive people. The pretentious, plastic suburbs harbor the same drive to violent acts that infiltrates the fruit pickers' camps and city slums. Only the external manifestation is different, and Oates unflinchingly raises and answers the question of why people are driven to violence.

In this series, Clara Walpole is a paradigmatic model. Her move from the squalid poverty of migrant camps to the wealthy home of Curt Revere is accompanied by violence at every step. The only way of life she knows is violence; the only avenue to self-affirmation is to destroy or conquer those persons who seem superior to her. From her sister Sharleen, her playmate Rosie, to Sonya, her co-worker, and finally to Lowry and Revere, she must either exploit people or defeat them in order to create an image of herself.

Clara's portrait, in fact, is one of the most pathetic analyses of the effects of violence on a human being. In her first appearance in the novel, she is described fighting with her older sister Sharleen;

they are "locked together in a hot inertia of hatred" (GED 22). This hatred, coupled with a hardness and bitterness, steels Clara for a life of hardship and tragedy. She leaves her father after he has beaten her one evening for being seen in a tavern and thereafter rarely even thinks of him. This shallowness of feeling is characteristic of all her relationships; her life has provided her with no models of deep ties of relatedness. When her mother, Pearl, dies, there is no mention of the fact at all; the narrative begins to speak of Nancy, whom the reader soon deduces is Carleton's new wife. Clara never learns to love; she learns only to use and to exploit persons.

Her moral education in violence begins with her father, who has killed a man. Few more sharply drawn sketches of a man driven to violence to preserve his self-image may be found in Oates's fiction. On Friday night, Carleton, having withheld and pocketed a portion of his earnings, goes on his weekly drinking bout with his friend Rafe. After a few drinks, a few rounds of arm wrestling, a few blows, Rafe calls Carleton a " 'hillbilly bastard.' " The narrative continues: "His big broad face was pale, the blood had deserted him. He circled Carleton clumsily, trying to move inward, and Carleton was conscious of being young and strong and handsome, and he could not quite keep distinct the image of himself as he must be in the eyes of the spectators and the image of himself as he was to Rafe, who knew him." This confusion and the need to preserve his image as tough guy relentlessly drive him to repudiate the appellation, "hillbilly bastard." After a few more blows, Carleton "felt the flatness of his image in the eyes of these strange people, who might have been watching from a great distance. He wanted to break through that flat image: he wanted to come alive to them." As they continue to fight and taunt each other, the narrative parodies the dancing of lovers. They embrace, Rafe holds Carleton's head "as if caressing it, a stroking of love gone mad." Even the repeated knifing is parodically described—"sinking in softly so that Carleton was striking him with only his hand, a gentle, slowed-down blow" (GED 38–41). And a man is dead.

Lowry continues Clara's education into violence. She recognizes in him an "invisible insatiable striving. She didn't understand him, but she sensed something familiar about the hardness with which he lived. It was her father's hardness brought into sharper focus" (GED 172). Lowry cannot live with tranquility—not even in nature. He is compelled to ruin the peacefulness of the river by throwing stones into it, as he and Karen walk along Eden River. With the same hardness and destructive energy he makes love to her that same day. "His face [was] twisted like a rag in a parody of agony" and she "felt as if she had been opened up and hammered at with a cruelty that made no sense because she could not see what it meant" (GED 189). But Lowry explains its meaning, " 'It doesn't mean anything except what it is' " (GED 191). No love, only cruel, violent sex. After a short, idyllic sojourn to the ocean, he leaves her, and she is forced to reevaluate and take charge of her life. By now she is so thoroughly schooled in violence that when she turns to Revere, she can dispassionately calculate what she has to gain from him.

As strongly as she is driven to exploit Revere, she must at the same time wait on his desires, prostitute herself, and forfeit her reputation with the community. When her son Swan is old enough, she instructs him in the violence she has learned. The promise that someday he will be master of the Revere household must sustain him through the troubles of relating to his stepbrothers. He is forced to compromise all his values to gain the promised bounty. But the one area he cannot compromise is his horror of killing. In the Revere family hunting is the mark of a man. Curt tries to make Swan a Revere man, and Swan recoils. When Revere tries to force the issue, the boy looks at him shyly; "he had the feeling for a moment that he could love this man if only he wouldn't take him out hunting and make him handle guns and kill things. Why was there always so much confusion and danger with men?" (GED 288). Swan teeters on the brink of love-hate, but having learned his early lessons well, he comes to hate Revere. Ironically, Swan, forced into hunting when he weeps at the sight of a dead squirrel, when he cannot understand how you can draw a deer at one time and shoot it at another, is involved in the mysterious death of Robert Revere during a hunting expedition. How responsible Swan is for the shooting is never determined; the only certainty is that were he intentionally to kill a Revere, it would probably not have been Robert.

Swan's ultimate inability to cope with his own sense of impotence, pathetically underlined in his affair with Deborah, explodes in his murder-suicide. Debbie, from whom he expects so much, only reinforces his own lack of self-esteem. She tells him frankly that there is nothing in him to love. " 'All my life I hated you but I love you too, I didn't want to love you. . . .' " (GED 430). In the end, "failure lay stagnant around them."

Used and manipulated by the people in his life, from his mother to his lover, he can cope no longer. Long suppressed, his violence erupts in a desire to kill the person whom he loves most. A crazed drive through the night brings him from the ugly hotel where he had met Debbie to the old Revere farmhouse, which for a time had been his home. Intending to kill his mother, he stammers to explain why, and no words will come out. Instead Clara ironically tells him the reason: " 'You're weak, that's what I know about you, that's my secret about you . . .' " (GED 438). But that secret had gnawed away at Swan all his life, eating away at even the modicum of self-worth with which he could credit himself. His next act affirms that weakness—he cannot kill his mother. In the last minute, he turns the gun on Revere, killing him, and then himself: his powerlessness complete.

Joyce Carol Oates devastatingly identifies the subtle, nonphysical violence in the vapid lives of the wealthy in *Expensive People*, the second novel of the trilogy. The first words of the novel, "I was a child murderer," set the tone for the fatal and violent drama of human relatedness. Except for the final murder of Nada Everett, there are no physical deaths—but the subtle brutality of their lives is murderous in its own way. The world of the expensive people is one in which children become alcoholics and dogs have nervous breakdowns, where one's place in the community can be estimated by the number of garbage cans, a whitewashed society with a brainwashed morality.

No less devasting because it is not externalized in physical acts of violence, an insidious impotence characterizes the suburbanites. Richard Everett early in life discovers that human beings are fragile glass who can crack easily; to prevent this, a facade of self-control and self-reliance is carefully maintained. When Richard, having been prodded into taking the entrance exam for Johns Behemoth School, does not achieve a high enough score for his mother's satisfaction (his I.Q. was recorded at only 153!), his mother insists that he take the exam again. Recognizing the request for what it is, Richard stares at her sadly, realizing that her every word, "every gesture, was phony as hell, and as time passed in Fernwood this phoniness grew upon her steadily, like . . . layers of fat. . ." (EP 79). He wonders if she can be rescued from this. The appearance of order is only surface; the mask of affirmation hides deep feelings of worthlessness.

Nada creates an image of herself out of her writings, her husband's job, her son's academic success. Her most characteristic action is backing out of the driveway; her favorite pastime, sponsoring cocktail parties. So superficial are human relationships that the Everetts cannot be sure a family in Cedar Grove is not the same family they knew in Fernwood. "There was a moment when they might have asked whether they'd known each other in another life, just a week past, but the moment went by and they were left stubborn and miserable in silence. They could think of nothing to say" (EP 30–31). On another occasion they plan to invite a couple to dinner—but they cannot remember whether or not the Veals had been killed in a plane crash.

Joyce Carol Oates satirically underlines the vacuity of the lives of the expensive people by their names: Maxwell Voyd, Gustave and Bébé Hofstadter, the Veals, the Bodys, the Spoons, Dr. Saskatoon and Dr. Muggeridge, the physicians, Mr. Grenlin, the Everetts themselves—Nada-Nadia who is really not Natashya Romanov but Nancy June Romanow, and Elwood variously called Father and Daddy. The Everetts live on Labyrinth Drive near Melon Lane in Cedar Grove, not far from Pools Moran. In returning to Cedar

Grove, they actually complete a circle of anonymous, plastic suburbs. The physical mobility, however, is only an analogue for the restlessness and insecurity of their personal lives.

The hostility of the physical environment is hidden behind rolling lawns, verdant gardens, and spacious shopping plazas. Plainly visible to the eyes of the child, however, is the seething hatred, the nothingness. Richard writes in his memoirs his growing realization that his parents hate one another. Engaged in his favorite pastime, eavesdropping, he records a fight between them and sadly concludes: "When all their stage props were ripped away, they always showed that they needed no fresh reasons to hate. They simply hated" (EP 99).

His mother fixes a "lovely mother's breakfast" for her "little prisoner" the day he is to take the entrance exam for Johns Behemoth School, and he vomits it up during the exam. Shortly after this, she leaves them—as she had done before—and Richard discovers "life without Nada was a surprise, because it was so much like life with Nada" (EP 136). Living alone with his father brings the boy to the disheartening realization that his father is nothing; the desk and pens, the buzzer system and secretaries, the titles and the promotions have not created a person. Unable to cope with his Oedipal guilt over his mother's departure, and no less affected by his increasing consciousness of his father's nothingness, Richard greets his eleventh birthday as his first deathday. His life at eleven becomes a living death.

The superficiality of the lives of the Everetts becomes glaringly apparent in the games they play with each other and in the delusions which they foster in their lives. When Richard's dachshund, Spark, is twice killed and replaced, the pretense is the same: Spark has been in the hospital getting fixed up. It does not matter if Spark is much bigger or less friendly or does not look like the Spark of two days before—the rules of the game call for a specific response: Richard will love Spark if he knows what is good for him. No effort is made to introduce the child gently to the reality of death, even if the dog is to be replaced. Richard learns that he must pretend the new dog is the old Spark. A similar pair of incidents points up the extreme to which this mode of avoiding reality can go. After Richard has succeeded in raising his I.Q. score to Nada's satisfaction, she plans an outing to the zoo as his reward. Passing a drive-in bank, they observe what appears to be a holdup. Three men rush from the bank, shots are fired, bystanders register appropriate horror—and it turns out to be the filming of a television show. Conditioned by the falsity of appearances and the blurred distinctions between the real and the unreal, neither Mr. Hofstadter, his son, nor Richard can identify a real accident on the expressway. Their immediate reaction to the smashed windshield of the car beside them is to drive on, convinced that what they had seen was a television show.

Perhaps the most hideous game Richard is asked to play involves his keeping secret the infidelity of his parents. Nada is not always backing out the driveway on her way to the shopping center, nor is Elwood always delayed from his trips by the fog. Richard must bear the burden of this knowledge as well as the emptiness of his being only eleven years old and, as it were, orphaned. However obvious the Freudian implications, Richard's confessed purpose in killing his mother is that he "had wanted to establish forever a relationship between the two of [them] which no one could transcend . . ." (EP 305).

Unlike Swan, his fictional predecessor, Richard is capable of killing the person he loves most—in actuality or in his mind. He believes he is the sniper who shoots at Mr. Body and missed, who terrorizes the citizens of Cedar Grove—who then must decide whether or not to have their cocktail parties if the sniper is still loose. Real or not, the murder crystallizes the superficiality and shallowness of their lives. The parties continue, his father remarries, but Richard is consumed with an insatiable hunger, an emptiness which he strives once and for all to stuff. Nada's murder is the one surface violence which erupts and disrupts the lives of the expensive people, but the undercurrent of subtle and erosive violence, like a subterranean stream, flows on, destroying human lives more tragically than physical death.

From the epigraph, ". . . because we are poor / Shall we be vicious?" to the explosion of the Detroit riots, the geography of the sources and causes of violence is mapped in *them*, the final novel in the trilogy. Unlike *With Shuddering Fall*, in which the natural world is infused with violence mirroring that of the world of human beings, *them* records the brutal malice enacted in the daily exchange of person-to-person. Focusing not on one family torn apart by violence, the narrative deals with the tragedy of two generations destroyed by powerlessness and the false belief that violence can be instrumental in bringing about any permanent change.

Modern tragedy transforms domestic landscape into wilderness, Oates writes in *Edge of Impossibility*. *them* is her fictive statement of this belief. Reality so bizarre as to be incredible prompts the initial reaction that this cannot be real, it must be fiction. Ultimately the author concedes, " 'This is the only kind of fiction that is real' " (*them* 11). Even a summary review of the violent events that take place in *them* defies the imagination: the murder of Bernie beside Loretta in bed by her brother Brock; her rape by the policeman Howard Wendall; her father's insanity and institutionalization; her husband, Howard, being crushed to death in an accident at work; her son Jules's burning the barn; her daughter Betty's pushing Grandma Wendall down the back stairs; her daughter Maureen's prostitution and near fatal beating by Furlong—all this in only the first third of the work.

Loretta Wendall is the invincible matriarch who survives the ever-increasing turbulence of her life. She is first seen as a "curly-haired little girl with confused impulses of tenderness and viciousness" (*them* 31). She never resolves this conflicting drive. Her initiation into violence occurs when her brother Brock, itching for excitement, kills her lover, Bernie Malin, beside her in bed. Brock is a killer needing someone to kill, and it happens to be Bernie, Bernie who had the mysterious quality missing in Brock "whatever it was that kept people from falling through the bottom of the world" (*them* 19). Were the senseless murder not enough, Loretta is raped by the policeman who offers to help her dispose of the body. They marry and for a time Loretta believes she has "come to the end of her life ... it was a solid, good feeling to think that she would probably live here forever ... Everything was fixed and

[52]

settled, good" (*them* 54). But life will ever deny Loretta this happiness of a fixed, settled, good life. She will be plagued with one hardship after another. Her spirit is undaunted. Unlike Oates's other fictional women who, unable to cope with life, succumb to nervous breakdowns, Lorretta is invincible. She refuses to "let them get [her] down." However shallow her personality, her dreams and goals, she can withstand the attacks. " 'There's not enough bastards in this city to get me down for long' " (*them* 157), she protests. The "confused impulses of tenderness and viciousness" remain unresolved throughout her life.

Perhaps the most repulsive and hideous aspect of violence in the lives of the poor is their unquestioning acceptance of it as a way of life. Even religious women who teach in the parochial school attended by the Wendall children admit it as a part of life. The principal, chastising Jules for smoking in the boys' room, resignedly tells him, " 'A certain number of boys must grow up to die in the electric chair' " (*them* 91). When one accepts that proposition as inevitable, all violence and its consequences fall into place. In *them*, more clearly than in any other of her novels, Oates reveals the impotence from which violence arises and the tragic end result of violence—impotence: the cyclical tragedy of impotence spawning violence which often yields only more impotence. A debilitating sense of entrapment paralyzes the characters. Despite the irrepressible need to put life in order, any effort to do so ultimately produces only a house of cards: their lives defy ordering. A malignant fate erodes their efforts, and every new crisis only triggers a more violent response.

Maureen, who emerges as the central figure in the drama, is the victim of her own inability to shield herself from her life. Jules recognizes in her from the beginning something different, something delicate. But one cannot be delicate and long survive in this nightmare world. And Maureen does not; she prostitutes herself in order to make money to get out of her environment, following Jules's example. She is not sufficiently schooled in deceit and cleverness to escape unnoticed, and when Furlong, her stepfather, discovers the money, he beats her senseless. For over a year she lives in a catatonic stupor, partially conscious of what goes on around her and lacking the courage to awaken in that world from which she had sought escape.

One of the first things she does after awakening is to return to school, to a night class taught by a Joyce Carol Oates.[17] She studies, but cannot accept fiction, because the "books you taught us," she writes Oates, "didn't explain this. The jumble was hidden somehow. The books you taught us are mainly lies I can tell you" (*them* 329). She reminds her former teacher how involved she had become in teaching *Madame Bovary* while one of her students rebelled: "*This is not important, none of this is real.*" And she asks Oates, "Why did you think that book about Madame Bovary was so important? All those books? Why did you tell us they were more important than life? They are not more important than my life" (*them* 333). She searches, desperately, for a way to take control of her life, "waiting for something to come to [her] and give a shape to so much pain."

Not finding that something, Maureen seeks other ways to escape. She moves from Detroit to a suburb, but 'Maureen' moves with her. She wonders how it is that her fate dooms her "to be Maureen all her life? It seems to her a mystery that she should always be herself, this particular person; there is no way out" (*them* 407). She proceeds, however, to make someone fall in love with her and she succeeds in seducing Jim Randolf, another of her teachers. Jim leaves his wife and children, marries her, and they start their own family in the suburbs. But Maureen has not found the key to escape, as Jules, when he visits, reminds her " 'this place here can burn down too' " (*them* 507).

Opposed to Maureen's delicate flight from violence is Jules's head-on attack. Maureen and Jules have much in common, as she identifies a certain gentleness in him, despite his mask of bravado. Earlier, when the Wendalls were living in the South, Jules had seen a plane crash in which a man's head had been split in two. He had run away and hidden in his fear and horror. Jules had learned Mama Wendall's lesson well, " 'You just keep fighting back. You got to make your own way' " (*them* 69). Loretta, however, does not understand his aloneness, "his being so unchildlike," his independence. All his life the twin forces of sensitivity and strength, tenderness and violence vie for mastery of him.

A very close call with death robs Jules of some of his spirit. "He'd outlived himself"; he wants only to "have emptiness in the midst of this city—to keep it to himself, but without selfishness" (*them* 445). But Jules gets involved with revolutionaries and with the Detroit riots. The looting, plundering, shooting only bring to the surface the latent violence of the city: it had been there long before the riots, seething, boiling until that moment when it would be unleashed on the city. And Jules, who had seen death so often and had barely escaped it himself, kills a policeman.

Life has made "them" hard and bitter people; it has taught them to fight and to kill and to destroy before they are destroyed. It has educated them in the ways of violence as a desperate but futile means of overcoming their own sense of powerlessness and impotence. Familial violence is only social violence scaled down and, conversely, the riots are only domestic nightmares played out on a larger stage. The root of it all is powerlessness: a fatalistic-realistic acknowledgment that in the end they get you, but if you run fast enough, hit hard enough, lash out strong enough, you can for a time put off the defeat. If you hit first, at least you have overcome passivity. The one thing "they" know is that when you are poor and powerless, you are also vicious.

Exploding from the first pages with the same kind of horrific violence of *them*, *Wonderland* repeats many of the thematic concerns of the earlier novels. In *Wonderland*, familial violence is at its worst. It includes not only the shooting deaths of the Harte family but also the even more horrifying living deaths of the Pedersons. The tragedies of the two families in many ways mirror each other: the strangling sense of impotence experienced by the fathers of both families drives each one to destroy his offspring.

Unschooled, unemployed, incapable of grappling with the problems and pressures of his growing family, no longer capable of merely making the effort to endure living, Willard Harte does the one thing he thinks will solve the problem: he destroys his family and him-

[55]

self. Precipitated by the proximity of Christmas and the closing of his gas station, his violence explodes into murder. He stalks the woods and fields behind his home in search of a way to resolve his gnawing sense of powerlessness and helplessness; not finding one, he chooses death.

On the other hand, Karl Pederson, the educated, established, successful physician, whose philosophy of life is "A *human being* ... *must become what he was meant to be*..." (W 73), admits his life is incomplete: he has been failed by his wife, Mary, and his two children, Hilda and Frederich. He sets out systematically to make his family into his idea of them, and when this fails, he turns to young Jesse Harte, sole survivor of the mass murder, whom he adopts. Pederson devours people: his wife, his children, his patients, and now Jesse. His monomania, while less dramatic than Willard Harte's, is nonetheless violent and destructive. His wife, trying to break free of his suffocating grasp, tells Jesse of the doctor's experiments, his failures which result in the death of his patients, his stranglehold on her. Jesse had begun to feel the pressure as Pederson had tried to make the youth over into his image, but Jesse's fatal slip, his sympathetic cooperation with Mary Pederson's plan to escape, causes Pederson to cut him off forever. "You are dead. You do not exist" (W 184), Pederson tells him in a letter. While Willard Harte's impotence leaves moribund corpses, Karl Pederson's creates living deaths: a wife and two children struggling to be free of his control, and an adopted son rejected because of his refusal to conform.

On his own, twice orphaned, educated by two models of destructive paternity, Jesse launches on a medical career and begins a family of his own. His medical education takes him to Ann Arbor, to the University of Michigan, where his self-reliance and independence all but destroy a colleague, Dr. Trick Monk. Monk craves the psychological, and possibly homosexual, support of his young alter ego, but Jesse's plans to marry and move to Chicago threaten to end this relationship. During Monk's farewell dinner for Jesse and his fiancé Helene, he reveals his tragic dependency and sick mind. Bent on a course of destruction, Trick starts a fight with Jesse. The beating leaves Monk near death and Jesse shattered at the power of one man over life and death. Trick's poem, supposedly written for the young couple, spells out the horrifying truth:

> *sparkling protoplasm!*
> *we are drowning*
> *it is like carbonated water*
> *it is like crystals baked into tons of ice*
> *we are drowning*
> *our fingers thresh the glittering air*
> *we drown back into ourselves*
> *into the shouting waves*
> *we are helpless as the meeting of two blank*
> *hot walls of air*
> *or two lovers pressed together*
> *in perpetual daylight*
>
> (W 255)

The metaphor of drowning captures Trick's sense of impotence quite aptly.

The people of *Wonderland* exhibit a new type of violence from that of the characters which populate the earlier novels. Until now, with the exception of suicide which Oates considers to be the "ultimate surrender," there have been no examples of physical violence done to oneself. Self-inflicted violence is punishment, not surrender; it is enacted on one's body in an effort to control it, to chastise it, to punish it for its impotence, its weakness. The only suggestions of this form of violence in the other narratives have been cases of abortion: Karen's failure to tell Shar that she is pregnant brings on a miscarriage when he violently makes love to her, and Nada Everett considers having an abortion when she becomes pregnant with Richard.

Jesse's wife, Helene, incapable of accepting even the thought that she might be pregnant, tries to injure herself during a physical examination. Then with her pregnancy confirmed, she fantasizes an abortion with knitting needles in the bathtub of a State Street hotel. But lacking the courage to inflict this on herself, she instead drives to the hospital to tell Jesse the news.

Jesse, whose skilled hands are trained for surgery, turns those hands on himself. Jesse has become involved with Reva, who is pregnant by some other man, and considers arranging an abortion for her. Tormented by his commitment to life as a physician, his own wife and children, the life he recognizes in Reva, and particularly the power he feels women have over men, he takes the razor in his hand like a "delicate surgical instrument" and slices his own flesh. Not unlike Richard Everett's shooting at Mr. Body, Jesse's deed is aimed at destroying physical weakness and powerlessness in the form of the human body.

But *Wonderland* seeks to outdo itself in tragic violence; Jesse's butchering of his own flesh and Helene's desire to abort her child pale beside the self-destruction which their daughter Shelley inflicts. Shelley has run away from home with Noel and both are using drugs heavily. Bitter letters to her father narrate her adventures with Noel across the country and the failure of her father's love. She tells him of her love / hate and her inability to resolve the conflict; she teases him to search for her. She reminds him of his stern demands that she and her sister be perfect, that they speak always in sentences, that they be not afraid or cry because pain and suffering are fictions. Her recollections add up to the hideous fact that he, in his own way, had imposed his will on them as Dr. Pederson had done to him as a youth, and as his mentor, Dr. Perrault, more recently had.

His desperate search for his daughter brings him to Toronto. "Jesse went over to the boy on the mattress. He stared down—his heart pounding in that slow, heavy, clutching way—and saw that this was not a boy at all, but a girl—her hair cut off close to the skull, jaggedly, her face wasted, yellow, the lips caked with a stale dried substance. 'Shelley—?' he said." When he entreats her to come with him, she tells him, " 'I am not here. There's nobody here . . . I don't exist and you can't get me' " (W 473, 475). Her new identity is "Angel"; her father is "devil." Noel, she tells him, has made her pure, and she has sought to destroy "Shelley" and create a new person.

While her father had done a similar thing in trying to invent himself as Jesse Vogel, Shelley's efforts to become spirit, to become "Angel," are the ultimate in self-destruction. When violence is turned inward against oneself, the nightmare reality has a power to horrify beyond any other outward expressions of violence. In *Wonderland*, Joyce Carol Oates completes the cycle of her vision of violence: from the simple and overt depiction of violence in natural and human life in *With Shuddering Fall* through the familial-social violence of the trilogy, *A Garden of Earthly Delights*, *Expensive People*, and *them*, to the violence directed at self of *Wonderland*, she has traced the root of violence to a sense of impotence. She has painstakingly exposed the source of personal and social violence with the objective scrutiny of a sociologist and the careful depiction of an artist.

When Oates turns her attention in *Do With Me What You Will* to other themes, a residual influence of violence is discernible, but the focus has shifted from the causes of violence to the effort to transcend and liberate oneself. Elena Howe suffers at the hands of her insane father, who kidnaps and takes her to California where she nearly dies of dehydration and malnutrition, and at those of her mother, who constantly uses Elena to better herself, marrying her off to Marvin Howe and virtually ignoring her the rest of her life. But the focus on violence is only secondary; the thrust of the novel is in another direction. Elena succeeds in casting off the effects of violence; she can and does liberate herself.

In this novel, Oates is not so obsessively concerned with representing the horrifying and destructive nature of violence. She does not mitigate the violence of the city or of human relationships in this work, but the emphasis of the novel is on Elena's successful struggle to assert herself. There is violence in the novel—kidnapping, murder, brutality—but it is relegated to a lower plane, it is secondary to Elena's deep, personal struggle to achieve a sense of her own identity and to fulfill herself.

The extra-literary but nevertheless inescapable question arises: can the use of violence in fiction serve any purpose? Is it merely porno-violence? Violence, Oates argues, must be precipitated in a work of fiction. "If violence erupts in fiction," she writes, "it should be the outcome of tension; it should not come first, nor should it be accidental."[18] Her novels translate this theory into practice; they are careful analyses of the forces that drive human beings to violence. Her works take into account the sense of impotence, the absence of self-affirmation, the failure to establish meaningful relationships with other persons which confirm and bolster one's self-image, and the ultimate failure to accept one's limited power.

When violence erupts in her fiction, it is not, as Elizabeth Dalton suggests, a programmatic resolution to every situation.[19] It is not Oates's handy way of resolving every crisis; it is the natural outlet or course of action her characters fall back on when they are confronted with threats to their self-image or with the exposure of their impotence. Violence in Oates's works is not the deus ex machina of an artist who cannot write herself out of critical situations. When Oates uses violence in her fiction, it is the very real depiction of societal conditions—as she sees them.

Dalton critizes Oates for "failures of literary intelligence, of structure and style,"[20] for not creating characters whose violent deeds are convincingly motivated. But this criticism misses Oates's creation of characters too simple or "ordinary" to experience deeply or realize fully what is happening to them and to society. Oates portrays the superficial lives of characters who themselves cannot be other than superficial. Jules, who particularly comes under Dalton's attack, is incapable of discerning—any more than he does in the novel—what is taking place around him. He is a drifter, moved this way and that by chance and happenstance. He may protest that he wants to get his life under control, but that is another futile dream.

The genesis of violence in Oates's fiction is scrupulously traced and nakedly described. Her novels may be so satiated with violence that the hoped-for purgative effect is mitigated, but the violence in her works is a reflection of the violence in society; it is not a violence in the author's head, as Dalton claims. The novelist does in fact "attempt to confront the chaos that surrounds us and yet defies our comprehension."[21] Repeatedly she struggles through her works to answer the question she poses in her review of *The Dollmaker*: "How can the human imagination resist a violent assimilation into such a culture?"[22] Her fiction pictures both the culture and the need to resist the assailing violence.

Violence, whatever its ultimate effect in a work of literature, must not be used as a series of set pieces; it is not merely depicted for its shock value. As Jules somewhat complacently remarks at the conclusion of *them*: " 'Violence can't be singled out from an ordinary day!' " It is a very real part of all ordinary days.

THREE

The tragic loss of community in the city

What this country needs ... what this great land of ours needs is something to happen to it. Something ferocious and tragic, like what happened to Jericho or the cities of the plain—something terrible I mean, son, so that when the people have been through hellfire and the crucible, and have suffered agony enough and grief, they'll be men again, human beings, not a bunch of smug contented cows rooting at the trough.

William Styron, Set This House on Fire

1

American literature reveals a curious ambivalence toward the city. As the setting for the New Jerusalem, the urban setting was at first sanctioned. Settlers came to the New England shores, eager to establish the "City on the Hill," eager to create a new life style characterized by brotherhood, righteousness, and community, determined to found in the New World a new place for man. From the first, the city was regarded as the ideal setting for community, for a life of shared values, mutual support, and encouragement, and in this vision of the city, the American experience was typical of most cities throughout history. Concern for city planning, widespread and imaginative among the settlers and townspeople of the seventeenth and eighteenth centuries, reflects the belief that "civilized life is urban life and that personal development in any full sense is possible only to people who live in or near towns."[1] While the urban ideal characterized the settlements of the North, southern colonization reflected a countertrend toward agrarianism. Thomas Jefferson, in fact, was an outspoken critic of urban life and regarded the city as detrimental to human development, although later he would admit that the city was indispensable to American life and propose a design for city planning. Most other antiurbanists also had to accede to the inevitability of city life in America.

Permeated by the highest ideals, these early colonists pledged themselves to unite with one another for the attainment of community. To live outside the city, away from the community of the urban settlement, to them, was suspect; and those who set themselves apart were regarded as renegades, deserters of the dream. There was little question about the city's being the proper habitat for man in the minds of the settlers: the city was a social and spiritual reality to be carefully tended and nourished. The newly established community would be nurtured in the city.

John Winthrop's "A Model of Christian Charity," written aboard the *Arabella*, first enunciated this dream. He urged his fellow sojourners to "knit together in this work as one man. We must entertain each other in brotherly affection; we must be willing to abridge ourselves of our superfluities, for the supply of others' necessities; we must uphold a familiar commerce together in all meekness, gentleness, patience and liberality. We must delight in each other, make others' conditions our own, rejoice together, mourn together, labor and suffer together: always having before our eyes our commission and community in the work, our community as members of the same body."[2]

Community, however, begs for definition. The Pilgrim fathers

[63]

defined the concept in terms of mutual obligation: "We are knit together as a body in a most strict and sacred bond and covenant of the Lord of the violation whereof we make great conscience and by virtue whereof we hold ourselves straitly tied to all care of each other's goods."[3] Here the emphasis is on the spiritual as well as social dimensions of the concept. Modern sociologists define community as the "interdependent collectivity of persons living relatively permanently in a geographically limited area which serves as a focus for the major portion of a resident's daily life; usually involves people who share common culture."[4]

Somewhere between the theological perspective of the Puritans and the secular perspectives of sociologists lies a functional concept of community. Robert French Mills, in his introduction to an anthology of readings of community, states that as a "complex reality" it is "not just a place, not just a social system, not just a way of life that is shared by a number of people that identify themselves with a sense of we-ness."[5] After an intensive study of the psychological factors involved in community, Seymour Sarason concludes that it is a "sense that one was part of a readily available, mutually supportive network of relationships upon which one could depend and as a result of which one did not experience sustained feelings of loneliness that impel one to actions or to adopting a style of living masking anxiety and setting the stage for later and more destructive anguish. It is not merely a matter of how many people one knows, or how many close friends one has. . . ."[6] Succinctly and incisively, Richard Goodwin offers a humanistic description of community as a "mooring for the spirit," an "institutional embodiment of shared human purpose."[7]

The failure to create community in the city is an irrefutable fact for which multifarious reasons are advanced: heartless commercialism, ruthless competition, constant mobility, personal alienation, poverty, and crime. In his significant study of the city, *The Urban Wilderness*, Sam Bass Warner identifies the three most cherished ideals of society as competition, community, and innovation. He asserts that community, the second goal, "holds that a successful city should encompass a safe, healthy decent environment in which

[64]

every man participates as a citizen, regardless of personal wealth or poverty, success or failure."[8]

This basic need for community cannot be overestimated. The absence of a functioning community in large measure accounts for the modern sense of alienation. Nothing can substitute for community, according to sociologist Robert Nisbet, nor can the quest itself be denied, "for it springs from some of the powerful needs of human nature—need for a clear sense of cultural purpose, membership, status and continuity. Without these, no amount of mere material welfare will serve to arrest the developing sense of alienation in our society. . . ."[9] So integral is the relationship between alienation and community that Norman Holmes Pearson sees the emphasis on the "agony of aloneness" in recent American literature as compelling evidence of the deeper yearning for community, a fact often overlooked in literary criticism.[10] Too great a stress on a sense of alienation has tended to obscure the more significant experience of the need for community.

Self-identity is not possible without fraternity. Not only does the absence of community create a "nation of strangers," but even more basically it makes man a stranger to himself. In the introduction to his popular study of mobility, Vance Packard argues this point persuasively when he observes that the "individual needs a sense of community. . . . He needs it for the shaping of his own sense of identity. He needs it if he is to achieve a sense of self-esteem and well-being. The challenge is to achieve a congenial balance between the individual's yearning for freedom and his urgent need for community and continuity."[11] Community, Goodwin affirms, is the "restraint that liberates."[12] Man inhabits society and society inhabits him.[13] So inextricably related are self-fulfillment and community that the failure to achieve the one is the failure to achieve the other.

The conflict between the need to establish community and the need for self-identity is mirrored in the corresponding tension between the interests of community and the dynamics of urban life. Throughout American literature ambivalent attitudes toward the city obtain. From the first fervor for a strongly knit community, the ideal rather quickly became eroded by self-interest. Despite the good intentions of the settlers, it was not long before the city came to be considered alien to the ideal of community and to its formation and growth: this dual vision of the city as a setting conducive to community and as an inferno detrimental to human life is not unique to the American experience. Moreover, the transformation of the American city from the New Jerusalem to the urban wilderness was latent in the very foundings of the cities. No sooner had towns and villages been set up than the movement away from the city began. This vacillation toward and away from the city has continued throughout American history, most recently evidenced in urban renewal and suburban sprawl. And the ambivalence remains: the city of hope and the city of despair. Yet throughout is the lingering fear that if the city cannot be redeemed, man may not be either. Harvey Cox warns that if we lose our hope for the city, we must forfeit all hope for man.[14] The hope of a new heaven and a new earth carries the burden of creating or re-creating the New Jerusalem.

Cox argues that the city is an ineluctable reality and that to imagine a better society apart from the reality of the city is to build a house of cards. This same theme runs through Oates's fiction: the drama of human life is ultimately acted out in the city, from which there is no escaping. Maureen Wendall's dream of moving to the suburbs to live happily ever after is shattered by the realization that there is no real difference between the urban and suburban setting. Sorrow, tragedy, violence, despair are not territorial components; so to move from the metropolitan jungle to the suburban Eden is not to remove oneself from these realities. This is why it is possible to speak of Joyce Carol Oates's fully realized sense of place and at the same time maintain that all her settings are one.

The very labels "urban jungle" and "city wilderness" bespeak a despair and a sense of hopelessness. The modern city is in deep crisis, according to Kenneth Boulding. "It is an aggregation of humanity that has lost its sense of community and cannot, therefore, provide a human identity." Alienation, rootlessness, and violence militate against the creation of community in the city. So too does the absence of power. Boulding notes, "We cannot have community unless we have an aggregate of people with decision-making power."[15]

Ironically, the city was founded as a protection against violence from outside. The classical cities were established on this premise, as were the early American settlements. From the woods and wilderness came attacks, evil, strange beings, beasts and beast-like men. Soon, however, the violence of the city drove men out from the city. Today, as in the past, men move from the city to escape the evil of the urban world. The dream of the New Jerusalem was always tinged with the reality of its flawed nature. However tarnished these hopes became after repeated failures to establish communitarian settlements, there appeared ever-new hopes of accomplishing the ideal. American literature from first to last is a recounting of this dream to establish a new society. From the jeremiads of the Puritan preacher-poets to the New Journalists, the impulse persists.

Adapting her title from a poem by D. H. Lawrence, Joyce Carol Oates in a surprisingly about-face article, "New Heaven and Earth," speaks out enthusiastically and persuasively for a transformation of American society, of her own deep hope for a new earth which, if it is anything, "is a flowering of the democratic ideal, a community of equals, but not a community mobilized against the rest of the world, not a unity arising out of primitive paranoia."[16] The new heaven and the new earth must be created by the stuff of this world and by its men and women.

2

Joyce Carol Oates's fiction, however, reveals the deeply rooted ambivalence toward the city which characterizes much of American literature. From Jules Wendall, who believes the only hope for the urban environment is to burn it down (*them* 488), to Jack Morrissey, whose legal work with the city's poor forces him to regard the city as poison (DWM 299), her characters learn to hate the city and to suspect its deadly effect on human beings. Her cities are the centers of seething humanity, of frustrated human dreams and am-

[67]

bition, where children learn to sell themselves or to be sold, women must prostitute themselves, and men become brutal, beast-like men.

The idea of a New Jerusalem is satirically undercut in many of the novels. Romantic dreams like Mered Dawe's of transforming the city into a haven where love and understanding flourish are countered by the more realistic and at times cynical attitudes of men like Morrissey. Bitter irony rings in Nada Everett's suggestion that Cedar Grove is a Holy City, and she is forced at the same time to say "all the world and all of history is a jungle, when it hasn't been a garbage heap or a graveyard" (EP 281). Her son's earlier reflections on the city of Fernwood anticipate his mother's angry comments. Richard writes in his memoirs:

> If God remakes Paradise it will be in the image of Fernwood, for Fernwood is Paradise constructed to answer all desires before they are even felt. . . . there is never any contrast between what is said and what is done, what is done and what is intended and what is desired—everything runs together. (EP 146)

Everything in the story controverts this conception of a terrestrial urban paradise.

Clara Walpole's garden is not one of earthly delights promised in the title but a jungle of nightmare and pain. Nor is Wonderland the hoped-for eden: it is a vulgar shopping plaza which images the market-place buying and selling of goods and services—and people. The cities of Oates's fiction are the antithesis of earthly edens; they are the settings for deadly power struggles between people, between classes, between races. And most tragically, they are the place of the death of the human spirit.

The city becomes one of the antagonists in Oates's works; at every turn it threatens to destroy not only human dreams but human beings. Detroit figures prominently in two of her narratives, *them* and *Do With Me What You Will*, and although there is no thematic continuity between the two novels—except for the setting which plays a significant part in both—the city remains the same. The

1967 riots of *them* have not transformed the 1970 city of *Do With Me What You Will*. A tragic sameness hovers funereally over the city. Oates herself candidly calls Detroit a "brutal city." [17]

Oates's cities are frequently the scenes of rioting by means of which latent hostility and burning hatred of their inhabitants surface. In this regard, too, her cities are all alike, differing only in place-names and intensity of feelings. Of all her characters only Loretta Wendall and Marvin Howe claim to love the city; she for the sense of wonder it inspires in her and he for its power. Tragically neither has good experiences in the city. Loretta, whose children become victims of the city, is forced continually to move deeper into the poverty and meanness of the city; and, although Marvin achieves great stature as a lawyer, he loses Elena in the city.

The city for most of Oates's characters, however, creates the sense of being lost in a crowd, of somehow being less human because of having been in the city, an experience similar to that described by the speaker of "Residence in London" by William Wordsworth. The crowdedness, the inhumanity of the city threatens to rob the speaker of those attributes of his personhood:

> O Friend! one feeling was there which belong'd
> To this great City, by exclusive right.
> How often in the overflowing Streets,
> Have I gone forward with the Crowd, and said
> Unto myself, the face of everyone
> That passes by me is a mystery.
> Thus have I look'd, nor ceas'd to look, oppress'd
> By thoughts of what, and whither, when and how
> Until the shapes before my eyes became
> A second-sight procession, such as glides
> Over still mountains, or appears in dreams;
> And all the ballast of familiar life,
> The present, and the past; hope, fear; all stays,
> All laws of acting, thinking, speaking man
> Went from me, neither knowing me, nor known. [18]

In the cities of Joyce Carol Oates, "all laws of acting, thinking, speaking man" are suspended.

Full of life, yet mean, dirty, and hot, the city in *them* is both a source of wonderment and terror for Loretta. Repeatedly transplanted, she yearns to set down roots, but her life is one of continual upheaval. When she is forced to move to the country after Howard loses his job with the police force, she is not entirely convinced by Mama Wendall that " 'America is really the country, not the city. People should live in the country. The country is a better place than that smelly city for a baby.' " Loretta's first month in the country is marked by a longing for the "lovely, dirty city with its municipal buildings of fake marble and its department stores and elevators and its scrubby open parks." Nothing happens in the country for her; it is spiritless—"out here there was good clean fresh air for the baby but nothing else. Loretta wept for her lost city and its dirty air" (*them* 65). Later that baby, her son Jules, would wonder if his "memory of the country [was] a fraud?"

When Loretta is able to return to the city, she moves to Detroit. As she enters the city on a bus with her children, she has the sensation of going "deeper and deeper but not coming to any center." Jules peers out the windows of the bus in amazement as no "map had prepared him for all these streets. . . . But he longs for the country, "where space was everywhere and there were no airless boxed-in streets" (*them* 80, 82). Taken together Loretta and Jules represent two diametrically opposed attitudes toward the city: despite the toll the city takes on her, Loretta enjoys the sense of wonder and thrill in the city, but Jules hates the suffocating city and dreams of escaping it for the "unmapped: wilderness of the West." As much as it can, Loretta's spirit thrives in the city, but Jules's is cramped and threatens to be destroyed.

Detroit is dangerous; its streets are "unflowery"; autumn has no effect on it. It is a "hole with a horizon." Jules could "smell Detroit . . . a kind of stretched-out hole." All that is ugly and brutal and impersonal is Detroit. Free-spirited Jules yearns for something else. After he takes a job delivering flowers, he reflects on the incongruity of flowers in the streets of Detroit. Yet, when he makes deliveries in Grosse Pointe where flowers are more congruous with the setting, a maid sees in him the "hungry look of a city boy." If flowers do not belong in Detroit, Jules, the florist delivery boy, does not belong in Grosse Pointe.

Ultimately the image of Detroit in Oates's fiction is the city of death, the place where human beings are killed and the human spirit dies. " 'Lots of people die,' " Jules remarks, " 'and in strange ways in Detroit . . .' " (*them* 271). People are gunned down in the streets of the city, but in Grosse Pointe, he ponders, they die "in hospitals, waited upon." Throughout the novel the contrast between the metropolitan jungle and the suburban garden is constantly invoked. Whether it be to wealthly Grosse Pointe or to middle-class Dearborn, to escape to the suburbs is to get free from the inevitable destruction of the urban setting. Jules's romantic dreams of a flight to California to the golden West are paralleled in his sister's escape to Dearborn—ironically, however, when he pays his final visit to Maureen, he warns her that Dearborn can burn as well as Detroit—never admitting that Los Angeles is potentially destructible and destructive, too.

Detroit is "always Detroit"; there is something unchangeable and tragically unredeemable about the city in *them*. Vinoba Bhave's refrain "fire burns and does its duty" (*them* 105, 503) which intrigues Jules from the day he reads it in the waiting room of the clinic, contains a hint of the phoenix image: the city can be purged by fire only if it is to rise from the smoldering ruins as a new city with a new life. While Jules insists on " 'fires [which] will never be put out,' " his associate, Dr. Mort Piercy, dreams more utopian dreams of society living in harmony, a city of peace, acknowledging that " 'society must be leveled before a new, beautiful, peaceful society can be erected' " (*them* 501-2). Together, Jules and Mort set out for Los Angeles and Jules's lifelong desire to go to the West becomes a reality.

The Detroit of *Do With Me What You Will* is tragically the same: the riots and the burning have not done their "duty." It

remains the city of murders and rapes and poverty. While Marvin
Howe and Jack Morrissey work with its poor and criminal, Mered
Dawe dreams of its transformations in love. The persistent image
of the city is the same: the urban wilderness where predatory man
stalks his victim, fellow man. Marvin Howe's repeated protestations
of his love for the city hint that the love springs insidiously from
selfishness. His urban clients feed his ego and fatten his wallet so
that he can live in affluent Grosse Pointe. His success and prominence are the direct result of the conditions of the city because
he earns acquittals for murderers and criminals whose deeds are
spawned by the city. Although Marvin likes the city because it is
"pure energy," not unlike his own tireless and boundless energy,
he chooses not to live in the city but to live off it.

Jack Morrissey has ambitions similar to Howe's. But as his ideal-
ism is more blatant—" 'nothing matters to me except people, like
this [the poor]'" (DWM 255)—so too is his brutality. Jack is
poisoned by the city, and his disdain for it becomes more and more
open. Although he works hard, he, like Howe, is motivated by
success: "And his victories in a way anesthetized him to his own
imperfections" (DWM 284). His is not a disinterested humani-
tarianism.

Unable to decide whether to go off with Howe's wife, Elena, or
to stay with his own wife, Rachel, and adopt a child, he blames his
confusion on the city: " 'the past year is all mixed up with this
damn city . . .'" (DWM 462). Their lives are inextricably bound up
with the city from which they cannot escape; as Elena gazes across
the Detroit River at Canada, she wonders at the people who might
live there, in "those houses that looked so distant, so safe, in a
foreign country and safe from Detroit—as if anyone could be safe
from Detroit anywhere anywhere . . ." (DWM 380). The city with
its contamination, its poison, is a prison from which one does not
escape.

Nor is the Detroit of Oates's poetry much different. "Nothing
can pry us out of here," she cries, "we are wedged." Detroit is a
"muddy vision of car lots and / car heaps." It is a "mad dance," its
crystal is "smashed glass on all eight expressways," and we are but

"protoplasm." The city is anonymous, "its name is not Detroit," it is "the unnamed city" where people drive each other crazy (AS 18–19).

Another vision of Detroit is suggested in her poem "In the Night." "In the heart of the city / is a riot . . .": the Detroit of 1967, the Detroit of *them.* There are "Fires at the horizon . . . a / human avalanche trembling," but it is a "city not a war." The poem uses the anonymous "they" of the novel and asks "What do they want?" The line following this question reads, "No need to ask. What will happen tomorrow?" The reader is left to ponder which of the two questions—or both—he has "no need to ask." He does know the answer. The final question of the poem, "Will they learn our language to die in?" embodies the tragic vision permeating Oates's works: they—the poor, the lonely, the unloved and unloving—need a language to die in. The language they learn is "our language" whoever we are who have already died. Perhaps they will die anyway, but Oates chooses to give them a language, our language, to die in.

The city in Oates always evokes the image of violence and anonymity. It is "explosions, sirens, faces awash / in the night's mad distance." "Yet the night / of the city," she reminds us in the "Unborn Child," "is close to ancient / night," the ancient night of nonbeing. Life itself is a cycle from night to day, and the city is part of that cycle. In fact, the "cycle is a city's night with its / casual deaths and its easing to dawn" (AS 33–34). Night and death and city are all immutably related.

Size is another factor in the destructive power of the city. In "The Seduction," the title story of a recent collection, Douglas muses on how much he likes people, but often "it worried him that there were so many people, even in this small city." He couldn't possibly know them all, or they him. "What missed connections?—missed handshakes?" (S 133) he laments. The city spawns anonymity, nameless people in nameless cities, missing connections and handshakes and a sense of belonging.

The city is also the arena of the inescapable fight for survival and as such sanctions the very fight. Cities, then, are to be feared and dreaded as places where one cannot live long without perceiving the effects. When Yvette runs after her husband in "The Maniac," she realizes the city where she had been living "was becoming dangerous, like a big city; like a real city" (G 121). The real city destroys.

Oates's Detroit is the city another poet-author has labeled "a horror," "the dead end of the spirit that says all good things come from stepping on another's throat. . . ." Daniel Berrigan reflected on the city of Detroit during an interview in Spring 1975, while he was teaching at the University of Detroit—where Joyce Carol Oates had taught a decade earlier. His reflections are echoes of Oates's descriptions of the city. Speaking of the unemployment problem, Berrigan noted a deeper issue, "the whole life of Detroit is ending up a junkyard, and the tragedy is that we're not dumping cars in the auto heaps, we are dumping human lives and declaring people useless. . . ."[19] Oates continually reminds her readers of this human junkyard which the city creates, of the waste and wasting of human lives, of the tragic holocaust of progress and technology.

" 'Everyone is anxious to escape Detroit . . .'" (MI 165), Stanford tells his young student Ann in "Extraordinary Popular Delusions," and the story proceeds to discuss some of the atrocities of the city. In another piece of short fiction, "Problems of Adjustment in Survivors of Natural / Unnatural Disasters," a divorced father tells his son during a visit that the child should be grateful to be living where he does because it's " 'paradise.' " " 'The city I visit now, the city I'm writing about, is really at war, and every night bombs explode, people are shot, children wake up screaming from bad dreams . . .'" (MI 115). It is a warring, nightmare city.

The picture Oates gives of the suburbs in *them* and *Do With Me What You Will* is more favorable than the one she gives in *Expensive People*. If her urban settings reveal the violence and hatred of the poor, the suburbs correspondingly depict the inhumanity and sterility of the rich. Her city dwellers are driven to rob and kill from a sense of powerlessness and the absence of a sense of personal dignity and worth. Similarly devoid of secure self-images, her suburbanites are nevertheless much more capable of masking their feelings.

The suburbs, so much finer than the city, breed feelings of superiority in their residents: Jack Morrissey glimpses this "ugly obvious truth" one day when he comes to the realization that the "world was surely divided into a great horde of ordinary people . . . and a very small number of superior people. . . ." He is haunted by this truth: "Once you were aware of these superior men, you could not forget them. Even in the noisy supermarket, even in the checkout line, this world in which no superior men ever appeared, even there you could not forget them. Even in bed, in the safety of bed. In the dark, all lights out except the helpless frightening lights of the brain: you could not forget" (DWM 198).

The revulsion of the suburbanites toward the urban setting is evident in Richard Everett's remarks that his family "rarely descended into the 'city,' " and that no "women ventured into the city" (EP 86, 151). Yet even Richard is aware of the deeper similarities. Driving away from the city, he and his mother observe "how handsomely Fernwood emerged out of the anonymous miles of suburban wasteland that lay between it and the city. First you passed a jumble of motels, gas stations, bowling alleys, discount stores, drive-in restaurants, overpasses, underpasses, viaducts, garished by giant signs of plump-cheeked boys holding hotdogs aloft, and one sign that caught my attention: a very American-looking man holding aloft a can of beer, with a puzzled expression, the caption being, *Read a beer can tonight.*" Not only are suburbanites superior to city dwellers, but there is also a hierarchic order of suburbs. The first, Oak Woods, proletarian, a "dinkly, arrogant neighborhood," is followed by Pleasure Dells, "as bereft of dells as Oak Woods was bereft of oaks, but decked out perhaps with pleasure." The next suburb is Bornwell Pass, which offers a shopping plaza "acceptable for certain kinds of shopping." However, it had only "shops"—not "shoppes" as in expensive people's Fernwood. Eventually they arrive at Fernwood " 'a lovely place to live,' " according to Nada. Residents of Fernwood are the apex of the social structure; they scorn the others, those with a " 'Fox Ridge mentality' . . .

a conformity of deadly intensity, a mediocrity which stopped precisely at the clean white-and-black sign which proclaimed: FERNWOOD VILLAGE LIMITS SPEED LIMIT 45" (EP 88–90).

People are bought and sold in the suburbs, more subtly perhaps than in the city but no less inhumanly. There is a suburban style of doing things, a manner of dress which identifies the suburbanite as different from the pedestrian city dweller. But the vacuity of lives is everywhere evident; the plastic suburbs produce plastic people. Going to parties and belonging to the appropriate social set are the all-important things, often the only important things. Behavior at cocktail parties is well-defined as pasted on smiles and handy compliments. But the growing emptiness gnaws at Richard, the "anonymous miles of suburban wasteland" make Vastvalley a valley of ashes, where all are "paranoid, all self-loathing and vaguely doomed" (EP 159).

Fernwood is the place where "all garage doors slide meekly up when their owners' automobiles turn into the driveway," where "no one was ever responsible for anything" (EP 164, 169). When Moe Malinsky, the visiting editor, tries to point out to the women assembled at Nada's that his experience of flying from New York to Cedar Grove has convinced him of the emptiness of the suburbs, his message goes unheeded. He tells them that "New York [is] a fantastic but utterly real city, totally integrated, totally alert. I flew out here and in two hours I can see that the suburbs of America are doomed. I am frankly amazed at the artificiality of this suburban world. Your very children look artificial, do you realize that? Typecast, healthy well-fed, tanned children with no cares, no problems, no duties, no responsibilities, no sufferings, no thoughts, children out of a Walt Disney musical! And these children are your products, my friends. Think of what you are creating!' " The only response this warning receives is, ' "That's fascinating . . . Is it tied in with your work?' " (EP 239–40). Malinsky delivers this indictment, ironically, between bites of jumbo shrimp and mushrooms, washed down with Scotch.

If Malinsky's comments fall on deaf ears, Richard, who overhears the speech, understands the implications. Sometime before this, he had written "all of Fernwood is kind, nice, generous, lovely, and it means nothing, nothing" (EP 143). As he fantasizes a painting of the "Abortion That Failed," which is himself, he pictures a scene of a birth. His description of the fantasy aptly summarizes his attitudes toward the expensive people. "Off to each side [of the painting] there would be troops of well-wishers that attend every birth. Bébé, Minnie, Mimi, whatever their ludicruous names were—I am starting to forget—and men like Father and Dean Nash and Mr. Spoon, men who are never naked but even in the presence of a Birth have their ties knotted up tight against their throats. And, everywhere the lushness and tranquility of Fernwood, approached by great expanses of highways, expressways, winding, soaring, veering roads that seem impatient with the earth, mountains of junked cars, beer cans, and broken glass. In the mist a half-formed, embryonic child's face, just the barest suggestion of a face, of a soul . . ." (EP 141).

The *nada*, the nothingness of suburban life is fully represented in Natashya, who is nicknamed Nada. She embodies all the phoniness, the superficiality, and the emptiness. Even her eleven-year-old son recognizes that "every word of hers, every gesture, was phony as hell, and as time passed in Fernwood this phoniness grew upon her steadily, like the layers of fat I have encircling my body" (EP 79). Her self-pitying self-indulgence is odiously transparent. She values nothing, loves nothing, seeks only to climb higher on the social plane. Richard's awareness of her superficiality grows, climaxing in his discovery that she is only Nancy Romanow from New York and not Natashya Romanov of European descent. She represents the fullness of artificiality created by the suburban wasteland. Equally false are the cities and the people of *Wonderland*. Not a utopia as the title might suggest, Wonderland is a tawdry shopping plaza, "cheaply decorated with 'modern' multicolored cubes and benches of garish carnival colors" (W 417).

Jesse's migration from the desolate Yewville, after the murder-suicide which wipes out his whole family, is not the first of his young life. Intuiting something is wrong with his moody, despondent father, he inquires, "Ma, . . . are we going to move again?' " (W 25).

The precedent for this situation has been to move, but on this occasion moving is not to be the solution. Jesse's father, incapable of coping with his growing family, his own inability to find and hold steady employment, the coming celebration of Christmas, kills himself and his family. Only Jesse escapes to embark on the first of many lonely pilgrimages to new cities.

After brief stays at the homes of relatives and at an orphanage, Jesse is adopted by the Karl Pederson family. At first this appears fortuitous for the young boy: a permanent home, a sense of belonging, the interest and concern of his adoptive parents. But the spell of good fortune is quickly broken. Dr. Pederson wants to devour Jesse, to make him his own creation, to use Jesse to "complete" himself. Just as a physician, he feels he owns his patients, so as a father, he owns his children.

Having so much wanted a home and a family, Jesse initially ignores the danger signals. As he had often longingly walked past the imposing Pederson prior to his adoption, so now he prays: *"Let me be like them, let them love me, let everybody know that I am one of them"* (W 86). Despite the cost to himself, the surrender of his own desires, his own personality, he wants to be Jesse Pederson, third child of Karl and Mary Pederson. Jesse loses all this in the bizarre attempt of Mrs. Pederson to escape from the clutches of her husband. The doctor disowns him for his complicity, and Jesse, about to begin his medical education, is orphaned a second time. *"A life seems to come apart, to be violently slashed apart. But then it comes together again and time resumes again; ordinary life resumes"* (W 187). Life in Ann Arbor is relatively tranquil and necessarily transient for Jesse. Completing his academic preparation, he moves to Chicago to begin his internship.

In Chicago, it is his task to heal the mangled, mutilated victims of the city. "It must have been the gelatinous air of late summer in Chicago, the murky humid nights, the teasing air of the streets, the itching in brains that led to such bizarre accidents—mangled automobiles wrapped together, workmen falling through the air, skulls split by playful gestures. Jesse's hands could not work fast enough, his mind could not take in all these people" (W 263). His sensitivity to pain and suffering, his sense of responsibility for his patients, drives him to seek strength and support from his wife Helene, who is incapable of giving him what he needs. Once again he is alone in the city.

Helene fears they married too soon. Too fragile for Chicago, timid, away from the safe security of her father's house, with the loneliness that is part of the lot of a young doctor's wife, Helene is ultimately unfit for life in the city. She becomes increasingly more lonely and bitter and silent; she fears being a woman and becoming a mother. The anonymity of the city has some appeal to her, for she "could lose herself in the crowds, walking freely in the crowds. No one would know her." She would "run, get into the crowd on the sidewalk, become anonymous" (W 274, 281). She enjoys the shelter the city affords from facing herself and coming to terms with her own weaknesses and fears. She both needs and fears the city. As she looks out on the city from the windows of a doctor's office, the window appeared "rimmed with eerie light—dark light—the sky outside had clouded over. In Chicago light changed rapidly. You could not trust the sun. It was hard for her to remember that she was in Chicago and not somewhere else. In Chicago" (W 275). Little by little Helene slips out of Jesse's life and he carries on an affair with Reva Denk.

The images of the city which converge as the novel concludes confirm the suspension of the "laws of acting, thinking, speaking man." Jesse follows Reva to an art colony in Wisconsin. His announcement that he is from Chicago is met with unqualified scorn. " 'Oh hell, Chicago is an evil city. . . . Up here is the end of the world. Your mind doesn't have to race to keep up with itself here because it's the end of the world already—everything is at peace" (W 367). A letter from Shelley, his runaway daughter, while not directly attacking the city, speaks of being closer to nature now that she is far from Chicago. She also reminds her father of a scene in a hotel lobby the day of President Kennedy's assassination. "Here in the lobby it makes no difference if you scream out loud or inside.

Nobody can hear. The screams rise in a pyramid but still they are silent, caught inside the faces . . . yet we are free here, nobody knows us, we are all children running loose without adults to hold us back, we see people who look familiar to us like people in a dream, but they turn out to be strangers—" (W 390). The lobby invokes and confirms the mobility and anomie of the city.

Pathetically Jesse pursues Shelley from city to city until he finally reaches her in Toronto, "a city in a foreign country. But it seemed like any other city. From time to time he caught sight of men like himself—men with suits and ties, yes conventional costumes . . . It did look like an American city after all. The faces of Chicago and of New York. The same surging flow of fragments, the same conversations half-overheard; maybe even another Jesse here somewhere, hidden by the crowd, on the other side of the street, hunting . . ." (W 466). The city: the tragic setting of loneliness and searching. Jesse's solitary pilgrimage from city to city in search of his lost daughter reminds him of how much cities are alike: the same anonymous faces, the same costumes and disguises, the same discomforting awareness of other lonely, homeless people..

Oates's portrait of the city is thoroughly consistent with the American experience. Hopeful expectation yields to crippling despair. The city harbors brutal men and dashes dreams to nothingness. It brings out the worst in men. Cities are dark, dirty, menacing. Only those too simple or too strong to be destroyed by it can survive; the sensitive, the gentle, the weak are destroyed. Yet there is a strange attraction about the city; people return to it again and again searching for, hoping for community. There is about the depictions of cities in Joyce Carol Oates's works the subtle but unmistakable suggestion that ultimately the city cannot be escaped. Therefore, if man is to survive in the city, he must be capable of redeeming it. Oates carefully identifies and analyzes three causes of the lack of community in the city: mobility, which creates a "nation of strangers," a lack of personal identity, which can only generate alienation, and the absence of any connecting ties with other human beings, which reenforces the feelings of anomie.

[80]

Defining modern tragedy as the loss of community (EOI 3), Oates examines the consequences of this loss throughout the pages of her fiction. One of the greatest detriments to the establishment of community is mobility, a constant moving about which militates against putting down roots and creating ties with other persons. Loretta Wendall's ephemeral dream when she and Howard are first married that she would live happily forever in the house they are renting, speaks to this basic human need. She wants to stay put, to make friends, to have a permanent residence.

Mobility characterizes every Oates novel. In *A Garden of Earthly Delights* the most characteristic setting is hotel lobbies. A more appropriate setting for the mobile society than the very matrix of transiency, the hotel and motel, could not be found. Karen and Shar live in hotels; they are constantly on the move once she leaves her father's house to be with him. The hotel suggests symbolically the impermanence of their relationship; they will never make a home together. It will always be a passing thing.

Oates employs this setting with even greater poignancy in *Expensive People*. Early in his memoir, Richard Everett hints at his parents' infidelity. Affairs of "business" are conducted in nearby hotels and motels. A second setting in *Expensive People* underlines the mobility of the society: airport terminals. Richard notes that his father has two brothers, one living in Italy, a second who, like his father, "was always being promoted and shoulder-tapped by other corporations, transferred and stolen and relocated back and forth across the country as if he were a precious jewel" (EP 24). The brothers rarely meet, and on one occasion he remembers that they had accidentally bumped into each other in the men's lounge of an airport. On their way to the furthest ends of the United States, they encounter each other at Midway.

The mobility of the expensive people is motivated by economic gains, which are coupled with a corresponding elevation in social status. Elwood's promotions involve changing firms; he rises from

OOP to GKS to BWK, names alone which suggest a mockery of system. The promotions also mean entré into better country clubs, invitations to better parties, and acquaintances of better people. Their social mobility brings them full circle: they begin and end the round of moves in Cedar Grove, of course, moving into a much better home when they return to the suburb.

Constantly moving about, not by choice as the expensive people can afford to do, the migrants of *A Garden of Earthly Delights* must move merely to eat. The Walpoles are forced to hopscotch all over the country following the crops. There is no opportunity for them to settle down in one place, nor to stay in any camp for very long. Carleton, feeling the pressure of this constant moving, thinks that he does not love his first wife, Pearl, because "love was something you needed time for, your mind had to be at rest for it . . ." (GED 15). The demands of his growing family, the need to move on, season after season, not only diminishes the possibility of creating any sense of community with his fellow workers, but also destroys the possibility of a deep relationship with his wife.

Carleton muses once that no matter how urgently he might need to get home, he probably could not get there. Going back home is impossible because he has no home, Carleton realizes. His daughter, Clara, comes to this same awareness early in her life when she responds to the question of where she is from with " 'Not from nowhere.' " There is nowhere she can call home, nowhere she can be from. But the basic human need for belonging, for being rooted cannot be denied. Clara yearns for a home. After she has seduced Revere, she ponders what it is like to have her name on a barn, a symbol of possession and ownership, of rootedness. The big, bold letters of the Revere name painted on the barn are in sharp contrast with the backwards six of the shanty in which she had once lived with her family.

For Clara, the humiliation of having no home comes up repeatedly. In school, which she rarely attends, she hears the word "house" and searches the reader for a picture to identify with the sound. The idea of a house, of a father in a white shirt and tie, a mother playing with a baby are foreign to her—they are pictures in a book, sounds in a reader, but not a part of her world. The unreality of it all is accentuated by the fake clock in the picture, a timepiece with no hands. Deprived of these things, Clara is forced to lie as she does to Rosalie when she tells her she had been in a real house in Kentucky.

Love is, indeed, something that needs time, and the frequent moving of the Walpoles does not give them the needed time. This transience affects Clara deeply: people move in and out of her life with great rapidity. Her mother, Pearl, dies and is replaced by Nancy, without comment; Rosalie, her friend, moves away and Clara never sees her again and "never said anything about her, but thought about her all the time" (GED 88). She even names the cat Revere gives her "Rosalie." Later, Clara, becoming Lowry's girl friend, seeks something more permanent than he is capable of offering to her; so she turns to the older, more stable, and settled Curt Revere.

Her past experiences have made her hungry to possess things, to claim objects as her own—not only objects, but also his land, his house, all that belongs to him. She bribes her son Swan with the promise that all the concrete evidences of stability, possession, and ownership will be his. The need to belong, to be rooted, still plagues Clara, and she passes these feelings on to her son. Although community becomes an impossibility, the external signs of belonging nevertheless are coveted.

them is also a chronicle of flights, of repeated dislocations. Not the dislocation of the expensive people where all places are the same place and all homes look alike, but the sense of homelessness of the migrants, of those who can call no place home. It is the homelessness that Jules feels when he looks at the Ambassador Bridge and thinks of the adults who could drive back and forth and "need never return to any particular home" (*them* 90). Howard's inability to find steady employment forces the family to be continually moving, which takes its toll on all the family, but none more than sensitive Maureen, who, after moving into a new house, cannot sleep for many nights. Literature has few definitions of the need for a sense of rootedness more poignant than the explanation Anse Bundren gives Addie for not wanting to move:

When He [the Lord] aims for something to be always a-moving, He makes it longways, like a road or a horse or a wagon, but when He aims for something to stay put, He makes it up-and-down ways, like a tree or a man. And so he never aimed for folks to live on a road, because which gets there first, I says, the road or the house? Did you ever know Him to set a road down by a house? I says No you never, I says, because it's always men can rest till they gets the house set where everybody that passes in a wagon can spit in the doorway, keeping the folks restless and wanting to get up and go somewheres else when He aimed for them to stay put like a tree or a stand of corn. Because if He'd a aimed for man to be always a-moving and going somewheres else, wouldn't He a put him longways on his belly, like a snake? It stands to reason He would.[20]

Man, being an upright animal, is meant to be rooted, to be stable.

The crucial question asked by Maureen, the victim of the Wendalls' constant dislocation, runs through Oates's fiction: "How can I live my life if the world is like this?" (*them* 330). Members of families, husbands and wives, are all alienated strangers. People without identities, feeling no connection with anyone, cannot create community. It occurs to Jules one day that the "tragic bridge between himself and his uncle [was] a bridge of kinship and despair" (*them* 344). When even the ties of blood are so uncreative, the possibility of forging lasting relationships with anyone else fades quickly.

This lack of love often turns Oates's characters into hard, disillusioned people. Thalia in the story "The Daughter" is overwhelmed by the impermanence of relationships as her mother, Anna, is about to divorce her second husband, Jake, in order to marry Mr. Harber. Reflecting on this, Thalia "felt dizzy, overcome by the riddle of life, by the mystery of love and relationships so abruptly lost, discarded. . . ." So painful is this realization to her

[84]

that she determines to love her stepfather, Jake, "to make up for what she [her mother] did to him." Jake, who has not seen Thalia for several years, is attracted to her youthful loveliness and comments, " 'so young, yet, so weak,' [and] in the silence that followed they thought of that: of weakness, of the ignobility of being weak, delicate, vulnerable to betrayal, loving rather than everlastingly beloved" (G 60, 62). In the world of Oates's characters, it is weakness to love rather than be loved, to be vulnerable rather than to be hard; life in her fictive world demands steel strength, receiving not giving, betraying before being betrayed. It is a cruel and brutal world.

Thalia's bitter defense against loneliness and hurt is hatred. She has schooled herself to "hate everybody, the kids at school and people in shares" and most tragically she confesses to Jake that she hates herself, most of all herself. Self-loathing and self-mocking are commonly devised shields against the pain of loving and being unloved in return. Thalia's crippling self-hatred ultimately makes her—like most of Oates's children—incapable of loving others. She is able, as the story concludes, to leave Jake and to return with her mother.

The urban poor are the tragic victims of absence of community and the lack of genuine concern. From the Wendalls to the Motts, the poor suffer from the cold detachment with which the machinery of social welfare runs, and Oates offers several critical indictments of the system. She wryly observes a client, Mr. Mott, staring at the papers on his caseworker Katherine's desk in her short story "Waiting" and comments "All Katherine's people were like this. Their respect was for papers, printed matter, records. They had outlasted other social workers and they probably would outlast Katherine. The flies remained" (G 263). Later when Katherine is promoted to supervisor, her work is even more perfunctory. "For years she had not understood her job, and then it suddenly became clear to her that the people, who were names in caseload files, were not customers; they were the opposite of customers. When the job was done well, the caseloads were lightened. It had nothing to do with the people at all" (G 274). There is no trace of human compassion or concern; the work is merely a job.

[85]

Katherine has no awareness of the power she wields over people, the power to refuse them money and the power to make them feel smaller than they already feel. More important she is oblivious of the awful resentment that builds up in them at the humiliation and degradation to which they are subject. So they wait until they have a chance either to get free of the system or get back at the system. Mr. Mott gets back at the system when all the years of waiting and mounting anger and humiliation burst forth. Mott tells her "I use'ta get there nine in the morning, when the dump opened. Then in we'd go—. . . and wait in line without being able to take our coats off, then around noon we'd get up past that whatdayacallit, where the chairs begin, then we could sit. And all them hours sitting there I just watched you and learned lots of things from you, like how to talk, and how to smile when you're really telling some poor bastard to go to hell" (G 281). Thus, the ugly chronicle of society's service and mercy is unfolded, to which there is no rebuttal. Katherine can only register surprise when Mott begins hitting her. Then she comprehends. She sees his lips moving, and although she cannot hear his words, she understands that he is speaking for all of the poor. And she begins to weep and knows there is "a lifetime of weeping before her but she did not know why." But she does know the "secret of her pain seemed to her to be in the long procession of sallow-faced straggly witches and broken-down men . . . but she did not understand it. She did not understand Mr. Mott's hatred and she did not understand the power he had, to make her feel such pain" (G 282). She does realize that the pent-up hostility of a lifetime will explode into violence; more tragically she fails to understand her power over the poor. The city has failed the poor—and Katherine.

The anguishing experience of aloneness is the secret everyone must live with, Loretta confesses. " 'But I think, what the hell, everybody is alone. That's the secret, everybody is alone and can't help it, like right here and now, in this place, everybody is alone and can't help it, like right here and now, in this place, everybody is alone and they'd all get up and walk out if they could and never see each other again. We're all like that" (them 499). The fear of

[86]

getting close to people and thereby getting hurt is very real, so too is the feeling of wanting to die because " 'everything is so lonely.' "

Perhaps the aspect of urban life most destructive of community is the sense of anomie generated by the environment. Nothing is less conducive to the feeling of unity and camaraderie than the anonymous and often hostile milieu of the city. Fear of becoming more alienated, of being absorbed in the amorphous masses of people, of losing the fragile hold one has on his identity is spawned by the city. The city often takes a destructive toll on human life. The city is not only alien to the formation of community but also threatens to destroy the very identities of those who seek community.

Her frequent use of the metaphor of china and glassware underlines Oates's insistence upon the fragility of her characters' self-images. She creates no characters with strong, robust egos; even those who appear to be strong are soon exposed as fearful, frightened human beings. This is quite recognizable in her male characters; from Shar Rule to Marvin Howe, her "tough guy" characters are revealed to be weak, insecure human beings. This type of individual in Oates's fictive world is incapable of entering a community relationship—even with just one other person.

In the case of Shar, every fiber of his being is threatened by the approach of Karen's love. She has tremendous power over him because of his fear that loving her, he will lose his freedom and his pose of independence. And once he realizes she does love him, the foundation of his false confidence begins to tremble. Marvin Howe, in many ways, is the summation of Oates's "tough guys." As a lawyer, he is a grown-up Jules Wendall, relentlessly attacking the establishment; as a husband, the composite of Howard Wendall, Shar Rule, and a successful Elwood Everett, he brutally uses and abuses his doll-like wife, Elena—until like a child, he reveals his "pathetic love" for her. His veneer of hardness and insensibility hides a child hungry for tender love and affection; but the brutality and possessiveness which mark their long years together cannot be easily shaken off, and Elena's new love for Jack is stronger than her response to Marvin's weakness, and she leaves him. Unmasked, he is helpless and abandoned.

[87]

Even the successful Dr. Jesse Vogel is basically insecure, with but a feeble hold on his own identity. Emblematic of his transformation from an orphaned waif in Yewville to a prominent surgeon in Chicago are the changes of his name. He begins life as a Harte, then takes the name of his adoptive parents, Pederson, and finally invents himself as Dr. Vogel. But his daughter exposes his mask. In one of her letters, Shelley recounts for him her reaction to one of his speeches at a medical convention. His paper concluded, he answers questions: "I watched as men priced you, Father. Added up your parts. They asked you complicated questions and you answered them slowly, carefully, Dr. Vogel cautious as always: such an expensive man! I wanted to put my hands over my ears, afraid I would hear you make a mistake. Afraid someone would attack you. I looked around and saw them all pricing you, adding you up" (W 387). The market place assessment of his personal worth is high among his colleagues and of this he seems to be aware. She continues, explaining to him what it cost her to be his daughter, knowing he is oblivious to this reality.

Back home, everyone knew what you were worth. Jesus, everyone knew. The kids at school knew, they knew everything, there was no place for me to hide. Even in the girls' lavatory I couldn't hide except in the toilet stalls. That's the last place in the world. When you are alone there with the door latched, just standing there, you have come to the last place of the world and you can't go any further. That's where you might go crazy if your head is uncertain. That's why doors should not have latches. Or there should be a back way out of toilets. (W 387)

Relentless in her revelations, she continues her recollections by noting that neither her father nor her mother made any friends. They did, however, have "valuable acquaintances." She cuts through the façade of his poise and self-confidence to reveal a lonely, tragic man.

Only when he is desperately searching for her in Toronto does it appear that he recognizes the truth of what Shelley has been telling him. Images of "a perspiring, overweight Jesse, hurrying to keep up with this lean, anxious Jesse . . . a scrawny, frightened young Jesse, hurrying along in this confusing tide" (W 466) pursue him. His next significant deed is highly symbolic: he strips off his "conventional costume," dons a pullover and khakis, and hides all his identification in a trash barrel. The journey that had brought him to Toronto, the sad search for his favorite daughter, begins to reveal to him his own true identity. However, when he finds Shelley she thinks he is the devil. His last words, " 'Am I?' " are not only highly ambiguous but also suggest that he has only begun his journey to self-definition.[21]

Another aspect of the absence of a firmly defined sense of self in Oates's fiction is the absence of a last name. Worse for Clara Walpole than having no home is having no real patronymic. When Lowry wants to test his superiority over her, he chides her with this fact. No name, no home: the two tangible dimensions of identity are denied her. These are also the two things he could give her but does not. Lowry asks her what she wants, and she admits she " 'doesn't know what it is yet,' " but when she does know she will get it. " 'You don't even have a last name any more, kid,' " he taunts her. She will get one, she promises him, even if she has to steal it (GED 137). And she does steal Revere's name. After she has convinced Revere she is pregnant by him, he insists that she see a doctor. At the office he registers her as Clara Revere "as if this were really her name, as natural as anything" (GED 239). But it is not her name and she knows it, which only accentuates the insecurity of her identity.

After the birth of Lowry's child, her realization that all people are strangers grows on her. The only person not a stranger is the baby. For all her sensitivity, her softening by love, she grows increasingly more manipulative of Revere. She has created in him a sympathy for herself by pretending to be the victim of his love. Unable to define herself, to discover and affirm her identity, she floats from relationship to relationship, a stranger to others and to herself. And in the end, she has no one except Revere's son, Clark, who comes to visit her at the Lakeshore Nursing Home where she spends her days watching television. She is ultimately alone.

If there is no perfect setting for community, there are certain conditions without which community cannot be created; these are a firm sense of one's own identity, a stability, and a sense of connectedness, without which community is impossible. If Oates's characters have one thing in common, it is a need for connection. The most characteristic pose of one of the characters in her short story "The Sacred Marriage" best depicts this need: "Howard was like a man in perpetual suspension—standing forever with a telephone receiver pressed to his ear, waiting, waiting patiently for someone to speak to him, to call him by name" (MI 10). He is always in readiness to be connected with someone.

Richard Everett realizes this need for connection in the early stages of his disintegration. He comes to know a "dizzying truth about human beings: they don't care." This knowledge is devastating; "it means something irreparable to know that," he continues. "Not just to be told it casually, or to be shouted down by a playmate, 'Drop dead, will you?' No, I mean *knowing* it, feeling it, tasting it with all your insides" (EP 55). Not something easily dimissed, nor shrugged off—the fear that human beings are not deeply connected to each other, do not really care, is frightening for an eleven-year-old.

Sardonically, Richard describes his family as having "the look of three strangers who have met by accident on a walk and are waiting for the first chance to get away from one another" (EP 20). Repulsed as he is by this feeling of not being cared about, he nevertheless does not hesitate to use his friend Farley as uncaringly. "I desperately needed a friend that wretched," he explains: "he gave me hope in the midst of hopelessness" (EP 83).

Implicit in Clara's entreaty for some goldfish is her need to be connected with something, something living. Despite Lowry's making fun of her, she insists on her need for something because she gets so lonely. She is unconvinced by Lowry's logic and deeply feels the need to be connected.

One of the factors which inhibit the making of connections is the difficulty of communicating with others. Jules describes this best when he overhears a conversation between his mother and Rita. "This woman," he realizes, "was saying two things, one in words, and the other beneath the words, and he was sure his mother was only hearing the words" (*them* 82). Because most people hear only the words, the communication necessary for community cannot take place. At the furtherest extreme of this dilemma is Nadine, who wants to live where no one can talk to her, who does not have the phone connected in the apartment she leases for her affair with Jules. Maureen represents the opposite attitude, wanting desperately to communicate with someone once she has awakened from her withdrawal phase.

Nadine's distance affects Jules, who misses a sense of connectedness when he thinks of her. He cannot understand why he feels so depressed "when nothing connected him to Nadine or to anyone else." He cannot answer his own question about what "human beings try to get from each other," because experience has taught him that people either hurt each other or leave each other. After Nadine walks out on him in Texas, he writes home: "*I have come to the conclusion that people are lonely, each one of us. . .*" (*them* 315–16). In a later letter he repeats his discovery "*that people have always been the same, lonely and worried and hoping for things, and that they have written their thoughts down and when we read them we are the same age as they are, its like time hasnt really gone by*" (*them* 326). It is the experience of frustrated anticipation, of waiting and hoping only to be disappointed.

To reach out for human love and support, to need the sense of being connected, is an essential human need. When it is suddenly shattered or destroyed, as in the case of Jesse Harte of *Wonderland*, the loneliness is almost unbearable. Jesse's secret return to his home in Yewville after the murders bespeaks his terror and sense of being adrift without a sense of connection. He longs first just to look at the familiar objects again, but his grandfather refuses the request. Then, one day he hitchhikes back to the empty house. His experience of "coming home" connects him once again with his family. He hears their voices; "he felt them watching him from the doorway, wondering at his being so alone, sitting on this crate." But he knows they have "left him and were buried in a cemetery outside town. But they were spying on him, about to giggle at his loneliness, his sitting in this back room . . ." (W 65). His emptiness is complete: the bitter words exchanged with his grandfather had severed that connection, and the visit to his home confirms the absolute aloneness he must accept.

Despite her angry, drug-induced abandoning of her father and her family, Shelley's letters are cries for the restoration of contact and connection with him. She defies him to come after her, knowing full well he cannot do otherwise. Her letters, which are in themselves pleas for contact, speak of her love / hate for her father. Despite what Joyce Carol Oates denounces as the moral ambiguity of the novel, *Wonderland* irrefutably underlines the need for community, beginning with the family. However imperfect and tragically unfulfilled the quest may be, the fundamental necessity for deep human ties cannot be denied. Whether it be Jesse's lonely and futile return to his family's home or Shelley's letters challenging her father to come after her—whatever form or shape the search takes—the need for community is essential to the human experience.

In fiction which explores the myriad aspects of this quest, Joyce Carol Oates carefully examines those things which prohibit the formation of community—mobility, the absence of a deep sense of self and of connectedness with other human beings—as well as the city, that setting, once ideally conceived as perfect for community, now regarded as a wilderness and a jungle.

FOUR

The language of tragedy and violence

But what must also be said, as we see this new structure, is that the most deeply known humanity is language itself.

Raymond Williams, *The English Novel*

The verbal ambiance of Joyce Carol Oates's works is violent. Her choice of images, figures of speech, and her basic rhetorical devices support and confirm her underlying concern with the violent and the tragic. Most activities in her fictive world are performed violently; conversations are angry and charged with hostility, the interaction between characters is often brutal and savage. Beneath this ambiance is the persistent and gnawing fear that one will be destroyed and the corresponding necessity of establishing or maintaining a sense of order and meaning in one's life. The resultant tension is electrifying.

A subtle type of violence Oates uses in her fiction is the deliberately annoying and disconcerting absence of a resolution in many of her pieces. The reader is teased into involvement with and concern for a fictional character or situation, only to be confused by an artistic statement which refuses to make sense. Oates acknowledges in "Fiction Dreams Revelations," the preface to *Scenes from American Life*, that art is often mimetic.[1] Because "nothing human is simple," that art which endeavors to speak to human experience will not necessarily be explicable or satisfying. Her own fiction, consequently, is often violently, annoyingly uncompleted. Her characters do not act; her plots are frequently unresolved; certain of her stories do not make sense.

By means of such devices as the imagery of shattering glass, of jigsaw puzzles, and of entrapment, through the repeated and powerful technique of describing even the most trivial objects and events in terms of violence, together with the rapid pace at which her tales are narrated, Oates creates her own unique language and aesthetic tragedy and violence. Careful always to skirt the potential dangers of mere sensationalism and horrific titillation, she generates an ambiance of violence integral to her tragic vision. She is thoroughly imbued with the fact that the value of aesthetic violence lies in its power to bring man to an awareness of his own mortality.

As John Fraser notes in *Violence in the Arts*, "some violences make for intellectual clarity and a more civilized consciousness, while others make for confusion."[2] If Oates's fiction leads to a sense of confusion, this is so in order to reflect the confusion inherent in human life and to push on toward a new consciousness. Only when one begins to ask how life can be lived or to wonder if a careless move can unhinge the universe can he begin to see how he can take hold of his life and avoid the careless move.

One mode of rhetorical violence in Oates's work is the technique of excessive concern for detail which creates an effect like that of a camera refusing to move to another scene; the reader is forced, as it were, to keep watching despite his desire not to see any more. This attention to detail, Oates explains in her review of Carlos Castaneda's *Tales of Power*, is part of Western rationalism. She describes this condition as "the system of perceptions and verbal descriptions of the world that, in our culture, is a social convention." But art is "not mere reportorial observation," because it "resists and transcends conventional categories of labeling, like Norman Mailer's poetic journalism and Truman Capote's 'nonfiction novel' *In Cold Blood*."[3] Although written in defense of Castaneda's works, the statements are equally applicable to her own writings.

In the world of her novels, people make love, play pianos, and eat violently. Music explodes, grins shatter, grease spatters maliciously as Oates uses every rhetorical device at her command to create an explosive atmosphere. By not relying solely on the narration of violent actions but supplementing this with rhetorical violence, she succeeds in generating a highly charged fictional environment. Her narratives mirror the turbulence and disorder of this nightmarish world. By repeatedly describing even the most ordinary of human actions in terms of hostility, brutality, and truculence, Oates creates a totally violent fictive world. There is no relief, and there are few comic interludes; once the tragic tale is initiated the tension escalates through greater and more tense scenes, most often culminating in murder, suicide, or riots. Infusing every detail of the narrative with violence, Oates leaves her reader exhausted.

She adeptly sets an ominous tone in the description of the night club where Shar, Max, and Karen celebrate Shar's recent racing victory. "Music from the jukebox exploded into the room. Mosquitoes and flies scattered to the ceilings" (WSF 143). One of their party is with a woman who appears "teased into prettiness" by "a violent, exotic outlining of her lips." Couples, dancing in one corner of the room, seem to "gallop together, violently" (WSF 144). The cumulative effect of these images carries forward the tension created in the preceding scene in which Shar has killed another driver during the race and prepares for the violence soon to come in the narrative. Oates directs the reader's attention to every charged detail as she describes even the most ordinary and commonplace things, such as lipstick and jukebox music, in terms of violence.

In one of the episodes just before Shar's death, a similar device is used. While visiting taverns along the beach, Shar and Marian

[95]

encounter a foreign couple shouting at each other in rage. The sun next affects Shar so that he begins to feel excited for a violence his body "craved and strained for"; then he is tempted to attack a young woman bather. Finally, he oversees two young boys "fighting viciously . . . with terrible hatred" (WSF 218). The mounting details help to generate a tension in the narrative paralleling the increasing rage in Shar until the "desire for violence had grown so strong in him that tears of rage and lust had forced their way into his eyes" (WSF 223). By heaping scene upon scene of violence—the angry argument in a foreign tongue, the urge to attack someone, the youths' vicious fighting—the episode creates in the reader an explosive urgency, the sense of having arrived at the brink of imminent action or disaster.

Likewise, the events which lead up to Nadine's shooting of Jules are described with rhetorical violence. Jules senses as they embrace that they are "fated for some final convulsion, locked in each other's arms, their mouths fastened greedily together in a pose neither had really chosen—like gargoyles hacked together out of rock, freaks of mossy rock" (*them* 314). The effect of the language, "a convulsion, kissing like "gargoyles," prepares not for a romantic reunion but a turbulent encounter. After several days, when they meet again in the apartment Nadine had arranged for, Jules wants to "gather her violently into his arms and penetrate her to the very kernel of her being, to her deepest silence, bringing her to a release of this joy. But she seemed to slip from him, too weak or too stunned, and he felt his love emptied violently into her again while she held him, her hands tight against his back, tight as if with alarm, her own body grown rigid at this crisis" (*them* 381). Nevertheless, Jules feels the moment is "magical." The effect of alternately describing the scene in terms of magic and violence is one of sharply heightened tension, and the rhythm of violence and magic parallels the mood of the lovers as it moves from ecstasy to terror, "making them both victims" of the "tyranny in the tension . . . between them" (*them* 397). Ironically, it is Jules who thinks he might destroy Nadine until he recognizes that her "beauty had gone all into hardness, in vacuity." When she pulls the trigger, Jules sees

[96]

the "sunshine shattered in the windshields of an acre of large, gleaming, expensive cars" (*them* 403). Her hardness, prefigured in the image of gargoyles, ultimately reveals her as a killer. Rhetorical violence, carefully placed in juxtaposition with the motif of magic, serves to create a tension in the narrative that far surpasses that which the mere recounting of violent incidents could create.

Clever punning achieves a comparable effect in *Do With Me What You Will*. After kidnapping his daughter and taking her to San Francisco, Leo Ross is more sick, bewildered, and frightened than ever. When he becomes particularly apprehensive about hiding out in his small apartment, he pockets his pistol and walks to the waterfront. Self-conscious, he is certain people are staring at him so he "shot them small half-mocking, half-inquisitive smiles" (DWM 33). The image of shooting smiles at questioning passers-by suggests how close he is to resorting to physical violence. He is at the limits of his endurance, so armed with his weapon, he shoots hostile looks at his inquisitors. Sometime later in a park, he wants to shoot the ducks because of their annoying quacking. Inarticulate, incapable of understanding what he has done and what is happening to him, Ross resorts to the only language he does know how to use: violence.

Even Ross's metaphor for the world is implicitly—and incongruously—violent. The world is like a sieve, " 'a lot of little holes that things fall through like water, like blood . . . like blood bleeding out of your arteries while you stand there and watch . . . The world is filled with holes that surprise you every morning' " (DWM 30–31). There is nothing in the basic image of a sieve to link it with bleeding, yet as Ross elaborates on his description of the world as a sieve, he implicitly creates the image of shooting, in which out of bullet wounds one's lifeblood might pour. The image is obviously incongruous, yet here, once again, rhetorical violence inheres in every detail, every image of the narrative.

Oates draws a second image for the violence implicit in human life and living from another incongruous source, from the fair. It requires a certain acuity to recognize that "things don't stay still but are always jolting you . . . . It's my burden. Things never stay still, it's like one of them trick rides at the fair—the floor starts tilting under you and you almost fall down" (G 96). However tricky the grounding is, for Oates what is important is the recognition of the tilting floor; the rest can be coped with, if one understands and accepts this reality.

Sometimes, however, the tilting floor upends a character. The process of being reborn, of coming to terms with life tragically necessitates a breaking down, a dying. As Lea Gregg and her young friends, in the story "Free," note when discussing their own breakdowns, they need a new term like "vision" or "penetration." "Because, of course, what had seemed to be a breakdown was in reality a building up, but before any building could take place the clutter of twenty years of buried life had to be violently swept away" (G 131). The past has to be destroyed—and violently—if the phoenix of a new life can rise from the ashes. For most of Oates's fictive creations the past cannot be built on, but must be destroyed. The possibility of redemption is turned toward the future and does not affect the past.

When Oates describes the difficult and often violent quest for identity and a personality, distinct and unique, she chooses to use the word *protoplasm* to identify the existence before the creation of personality. One of the earliest uses of the word occurs in Trick Monk's poetry where it is quite in keeping with the character's nonidentity. However, to be reborn in Oates's recent fiction means to achieve one's sense of meaning, one's personality for the anonymous "protoplasm" of the present. Neil Myer, a young orderly in "Narcotic," grapples with this process when he visits a former patient, a girl who had tried to commit suicide. Besieged by doubts of his own identity, he longs to tell her of the "taunting voice in his head that told him he was *Neil Myer* and could not escape. A teaspoon of protoplasm?" (G 316). Groping for his identity, he can only find his name. And he knows "his name is not important, but sometimes he discovered himself repeating it, over and over, mechanically fascinated by its sound. *Neil Myer.* A combination of shrill shrieking sounds that were muffled by the 'N' and the 'M' but were not really silenced" (G 305).

[98]

When he leaves the hospital on his way to visit Paula, the young girl, he feels the people he passes on the street are accusing him: "*You are still Neil Myer.*" When he fantasizes making love to her, he imagines "a time when he would not be *Neil Myer* but an anonymous young man, twenty-six years old, in anonymous good health, making love to an anonymous young woman" (G 313). Neil is caught trying to wrest his personality, his identity, from the teaspoon of protoplasm which is his existence and, at the same time, trying to escape that identity through anonymity.

In addition to the direct, overt use Joyce Carol Oates makes of violence are the subtle, pervasive suggestions of violence. The very pace of her narratives leaves the reader breathless; she creates a "pitch close to madness.' "[4] In just more than ten pages of the first chapter of A *Garden of Earthly Delights*, there is a collision between a truck of migrants and an auto, an angry fight between the two drivers, and the birth of a child. The rapid-fire telling of the events sets a pace which mirrors the frenzied activity of the lives of the characters. In *With Shuddering Fall*, the opening pages describe the cruel domestic setting from which Karen Herz inevitably must escape. *them* narrates in the first fifty pages the senseless murder of a young boy, the depressing domestic conditions of the Botsford family, and Loretta's rape by a policeman. Likewise, *Wonderland* recounts a mass murder and suicide all in its first two chapters. Not only are the events in themselves violent, but the very manner and speed with which they are narrated increase and tighten the tension. Critics have remarked that any synopsis of an Oates novel is practically impossible because there is a density of episodes that makes it difficult to recall and separate one event from another. These rhetorical techniques—the rapid pacing of the narration and the infusion of violence into detail—create an atmosphere of unrelieved tension: the incremental effect creates a totally violent fictive ambiance.

By her constant use of inversions and juxtapositions, Oates is implicitly violent. By equating totally dissimilar objects, she forces her reader to reexamine not only the objects themselves but the very language which can create such incongruity. " 'Bombs are poetry

when they go off. Machine-gun fire is poetry. Agony is poetry' "—
so Lea is told by one of her friends. "Life," on the other hand, "is
ugly" (G 141). By distorting the commonplace in the heinous and
the ugly into the artful, Oates constantly affects the reader's sensi-
bilities. The marked difficulty of accepting these inversions helps
to unsettle the reader's convictions about the ugly, about poetry,
about life—the very effect Oates set about to generate. Finally, she
calls into question language itself which can distort and misrep-
resent. As one of her characters bewilderedly explains, "telling
[the truth] was an act of violence" (G 125). Telling the truth is
the ultimate aim of Oates's fiction—however violent, however un-
pleasant and distasteful, however cruel and brutal that truth is.

Perhaps the most successful images suggesting the fragility of
human life assailed on every side by violence are those of fine glassware and china. Reminiscent of a similar use of the images by
Tennessee Williams in *The Glass Menagerie*, Oates's characters
are often described in terms of fracturing or shattering glassware.
The sense of holding onto one's life delicately but firmly, of trying
to prevent the breakage, is poignantly captured in Jules Wendall's
remarks to Nadine. Reunited after a nine-year separation, he con-
fides to her that one thing he had come to realize during his con-
valescence is that " 'we all carried ourselves like glass, we are very
breakable' " (*them* 363). In his short lifetime he had come to
understand how very fragile a hold a human being can have on his
own life and destiny, how much he is the victim of the violence
and cruelty of others. He is not the complete master of his life; he
never has the total control over his life which he constantly seeks.
When he was only eighteen and had come to visit Maureen after
her beating by Furlong, he had already experienced the unspoken
feeling of his own fragility; "he carried himself up into this apartment like a man carrying something breakable" (*them* 223). This
feeling of being breakable is his throughout his life.

As Richard Everett moves more and more into his tale, the awareness of his frailty grows on him. But the image of destructibility is
more devastating in this narrative than in the others because the
relief of "falling apart" is denied. Richard writes, "I am glass,

transparent and breakable as glass, but—and this is the tragedy—
we who are made of glass may crack into millions of jigsaw pieces
but we do not fall apart. We never fall apart. Instead we keep
lumbering around and talking. We want nothing more than to fall
apart, to disintegrate, to be released into a shower of slivers and
have done with it all, but the moment is hard to come by, as you
can see" (EP 101). The escape, the "having done with it all," the
merciful respite of forgetfulness and disintegration are withheld;
the anguish and the pain of enduring as a million jagged jigsaw
pieces remain.

The image of breaking or shattering into pieces is most frequently
used in relation to facial expressions and suggests a fragile mask.
As Carleton stands by, waiting as his wife delivers their child, he
steels himself not to betray any emotion. He cannot show too much
concern for his wife; men are not supposed to do that. But when
she screams with the pains of labor, he must redouble his efforts
"to keep his face from breaking into pieces" (GED 13). The image
of fracturing, of being tested to the point of breaking, to a point
beyond one's endurance, captures the tension of the moment.
Carleton fears the breaking of his mask, the exposing of his feelings.

Clara, his daughter, experiences a similar tension of preserving
her mask when she and Rosalie are on their little excursion to the
town on Rosalie's birthday. Faced with the wonder of things she
had never seen before, Clara starts to cry and feels her face breaking up into pieces. She needs to destroy the order and peace, the
prosperity she finds in the town. Resisting the temptation to break
the stained glass windows of a storybook house, she contents herself with stealing an American flag from the porch. Ironic as that
gesture is—two poor migrant children stealing a flag from the home
of more prosperous citizenry—it gives the girls great delight, and
Clara runs off triumphantly with her prize.

The ability to keep her face from breaking into pieces requires
great inner control. It also requires that Clara know what face to
wear; it requires that she be able to judge which mask is appropriate
to the occasion. Most of her life, Clara is plagued with the problem
of deciding on the right face. Often, particularly during the early

[101]

days of her relationship with Lowry, she confesses how hard it is "to know what kind of a face to have" (GED 150). Clara's challenge is to determine on and then to wear the right face for Lowry: the face that will keep him. So she must search for the right mask. The only time her expression is described as soft is in a photo taken on their trip to the shore. Clara's picture is vague "with a kind of beauty never hers ... her face misty and softened by some mistake in the photographing process" (GED 195). A soft countenance could only be a mistake; Clara knows too well not to wear such a face.

Clara's fictional ancestor, Karen Herz, is actually called a "little mask" when Max knowingly tells her that he recognizes the fact she had been pampered during her life and could consequently manipulate people. She had not fooled him, however; he knows her tricks. Despite her being "very discreet and learned" (WSF 88), she is a little "persona" which Max thoroughly enjoys.

The masks, the "faces of all the world," appear to Maureen Wendall to be "frozen hard into expressions of cunning and anger." Sensitive, gentle Maureen, "having no hardness in her," is forced to creep into silence where she can wait for the day "when everything would be orderly and neat, when she could arrange her life the way she arranged the kitchen after supper, and she too might be frozen hard, fixed, permanent, beyond their ability to hurt" (*them* 136). Maureen is too simple and guileless to protect herself. Because she does not or cannot become "frozen hard," she constantly teeters on the brink of "breaking into pieces" (*them* 202). When she finally does break, she retreats behind an impenetrable wall of silence. Openness and tenderness leave her too vulnerable; as Maureen tragically learns, one can too easily be broken when one does not wear the right mask.

Forced into fashion modeling to help support her mother, young Elena Ross is taught early in life that she must "*take care of that face, carry it like a crystal*" (DWM 79). She must keep her mask in place, her smile ready. Not only does the image of carrying a crystal fittingly depict the care and attention necessary to have an acceptable "face," but it also suggests Elena's various refractions of personality. Deprived of a childhood by her mother's ambitions, she is quickly married off to Marvin Howe, whom she not only does not love, but whom she does not even know. The model her mother, Ardis, offers of a confident and self-assured adult is anything but imitable: Ardis changes her name six times, undergoes plastic surgery, is continually dyeing her hair. When one's physical identity is so changeable, one's own deeper sense of identity is undoubtedly unstable. Ardis's advice to her daughter to carry herself like crystal is appropriate to the kind of life Elena is destined to lead. She must be equipped to wear many masks—until she finally does not know who she is and does not want to live. It is no wonder that with her recounting of her temptation to commit suicide at fourteen comes the recollection of her feelings of freedom. She had pricked her wrist with a paring knife and she *"never forgot that pinprick sharp as a flash of light: freedom"* (DWM 309). When Jack Morrissey finds her in a trancelike state in front of a statue, she recalls withdrawing into peace, going into stone like the statue, but having to awake and to live. She is confused and fantasizes her own death as a way out. She has worn so many masks that her real identity has become obscured, and death looks like a long sought-after release.

Elena's fragility is almost comically noted when Jack, with a "stricken, questioning look," checks to see that she is not hurt, not damaged after they have intercourse. She is used to this kind of inspection by her husband, Marvin. Living on the brink of *"nullity"* and *"extinction,"* she needs to be constantly monitored—both her husband and her lover identify this weakness in her.

The continual suggestions of fragility and weakness, the metaphors of china and glassware, the hints of personalities shattering and breaking into pieces serve well to intensify the ambiance of violence in Joyce Carol Oates's fiction. She deftly sketches in the personalities of characters brought to the very brink of destruction and despair—all of which she skillfully works into her tales of unspeakable violence, with the effect of creating a fictive world in which violence inheres in even the most quotidian details. On occasion, she appears to mute the shocking effects of violence by draping the scenes in terms of magic. However, rather than muting the violence, the use of magic only more dramatically points to its horror.

In what is perhaps one of the most horribly explicit scenes in all of Oates's fiction—Brock's shooting to death Loretta's boyfriend beside her in bed—she has Loretta muse in stunned wonderment that "one shot had done it, like magic" (*them* 38). Incomprehensible as that event is, Loretta can only grasp its significance when she thinks of it as magic: time seems stopped; the room becomes unfamiliar. The only way she can cope with the reality is to regard it initially as magic. Gradually, however, the realization of what has happened descends on her, and she must act. Her own sense of the unreality of the situation is reenforced by the fact that the one magical shot arouses no response in anyone else. "Maybe a gunshot in the middle of the night wasn't much of a surprise after all" (*them* 37), she reflects. In stunned bewilderment, the sixteen-year-old girl must try to get her wits together and handle the situation.

Young Richard Everett speaks ironically of magic in his tale. His sense of how certain things happened "magically" belies his childlike candor and points to a fierce cynicism. When he introduces his parents into the narrative, his wry observation captures his love-hate attitude toward them: the love is magic, the hate, real. He writes, "at these special times when we were together I thought I had somehow, magically, captured a man and a woman from another land, foreign and exotic and not quite speaking my language, who were tamed by my power and love and who walked obediently after me ... These were my true parents. The others—the dissatisfied Natashya Romanov, minor writer, and the blubbering breast-beating executive Elwood Everett—were nothing but cruel stepparents" (EP 22). Another time he describes his home as having at times a "certain soft magic, misty air" (EP 64). When things are well between his parents and between them and him, the times are like a magical dream. Yet he is fully aware that nothing is magic, so that rather than mute the horror of his story, his descriptions of magical events and situations only serve to call greater attention to the violence and chaos of his life. A departure from Oates's straightforward, stranger-than-fiction "histories," this novel parodies the creation of a novel. In so doing, those events and deeds of violence so horrifying in her other works are minimized and seemingly discredited. The underlying question of whether or not Richard actually murders his mother is never resolved and ultimately ceases to be a significant question.

With ever-greater irony, in *them*, Jules is described as a magician. As a youth, his "magic words" can make his companions perform anything he suggests. Even when it seems that nothing will ever be right in his life, he retains his belief in his magic touch. But as Maureen puzzles over his near-fatal shooting by Nadine, she comes to realize that there is no magic in America where "it wears out too quickly." She equates magic with life, being, identity, "the mysterious substance of the eye," and she is forced to conclude that it is a "terrible cruelty, because it wears out. In America it wears out quickly" (*them* 410). Magic cannot exist in her country—it is too easily killed off and destroyed.

In *Wonderland*, too, Oates ironically uses the make-believe magical world to suggest the muting of violence. The very title conveys the image of unreality and fantasy.[5] Occasional references to magic in the text inversely impute horror—not wonder—to the incidents. The ego-maniacal Dr. Pederson declares in a guest sermon he delivers in the local church that "there is something magical about the United States. This is a time of magic...." (*W* 113). Jesse Harte, his adopted son, is seated in the congregation and caught up with the meaning of these words. He tries to make sense of them, turning them over in his mind. For a fleeting period of his life, things do seem magical, but the spell is quickly broken when he is cast off by Pederson and declared dead. There is no magic, no wonder in Jesse's life, only horror and pain.

Another effective device Oates uses is stark and often repulsive realism, as in the story, "Did You Ever Slip on Red Blood?" Like a refrain, the question is repeated throughout the narrative. The short fiction opens with the query, the meaning of which, again in typical Oates fashion, is only revealed at the end of the narration. Allusions to death and to a killing fill the pages of the story in a disconcerting and unsatisfying fashion and are only fully explained

[105]

in retrospect. When Oberon and Marian are first described, Oberon looks at her as if [she were] centered in the telescopic sight of a rifle" (MI 339) which, one later learns, is exactly how he first saw her.

Throughout the narrative, Marian compulsively asks Oberon if he had ever slipped on red blood as she had, the red blood of the man he had shot. Marian believes that she loved Robert Severin, a man she had just met, the slain hijacker. And, as could only happen in Oates's world, Marian, the stewardess, and Oberon, the FBI agent, two lonely people, eventually get together, and believing they are in love, have an affair. Every element of the narrative creates a tension; not only the rifle, the flare which looks like a stick of dynamite, the pocket knife, but also the more subtle things like the anonymity secured through the use of sunglasses or the growing of a beard, the flight to strange cities and foreign countries, and the deep loneliness that makes strangers instant lovers. A master craftsman, Oates introduces no detail into the story that does not advance or increase the tension. Even the time sequence of the fiction is unsatisfyingly disjointed; nothing makes sense until the end, but at least in this narrative, the various elements fall into place at the conclusion. The red blood on which Marian slips is ironically—and tragically—that of a young, confused pacifist.

The fine fusion of intention and description at which Oates is so skilled is everywhere manifest in her writings. The opening story of her most recent collection of short fiction recapitulates the problem of anonymity, a theme often repeated in the volume, and does so most effectively by means of her use of rhetorical techniques and devices. The characters and setting of "The Girl" do not have names, but labels: The Director, the Cop, the Motorcyclist, the Beach, the Girl. Persons do not have identities; they merely represent functions. Nor do they relate to one another; they are only actors in a bizarre scenario. The story concerns events surrounding the making of a film during which the Girl is gang banged. When she sees the Director, some time after the filming, and tries to address him in the street, he is described as machine-like: a "kind of shutter clicked in his head" (G 13). He seems not to remember her, but she needs the assurance that the film-making had been real, that she had not imagined it, that she was the star. So out of touch with reality is she that her concern is only to establish her role in the film. Mechanical people look at each other "like on film," and people walk past them in the street as passersby "in a movie." "They are not in focus"; they are as blurred as are the events and circumstances of the story.

The story is filled with the lack of concern for and the failure to understand the effect one person has on another. The need for acceptance and sensitivity is nowhere in the story more pathetically described than when the Director blurts out, " 'I'm an orphan. . . . I'm from a Methodist orphanage in Seattle' " (G 8). In response, the Cop grins and the Motorcyclist laughs. The Director's pathetic confession and the Girl's later cry for recognition are the products of the anomie of society. And Oates draws attention to this central issue through her rhetorical device of not naming her characters and of vaguely blurring the action.

Set against the fierce images of violence, the most frequent image of order and tranquility is the library. Neat, orderly and ordered rows of books stand in sharp contrast with the chaos and disorder of the world outside the library. While Karen recovers from her strange illness, Max brings her magazines and books from the local library. In her mind the library is a component of the systematic structure of city government: the order of the library is a microcosm of the system of the city. When she sees the books that Max had "checked out of the library in the city, she was struck by a sense of disorder, of wonder as if it were somehow absurd to have to see her bed and this anonymous room in relation to a larger city, a coherent world of governmental design that in turn related itself to the world of her family (WSF 163–64). The library books suggest the apparent larger order of the world outside and sharply remind Karen of the disorder of her life.

Maureen Wendall in the novel *them*, however, is more obsessively fascinated with the order of the library. Early in her life, the library had become a shelter and source of solitude. After she awakens from the catatonic stupor brought on by her near-fatal beating by Furlong, she again retreats to the quiet security of the library. She senses the world is "out of control, crazy"; only the library affords peace, tranquility, and order, a respite from the disorder of daily life. Suspicious that the other patrons of the library would like to "throw the books out the windows, break the lamps and chairs, hit one another over the head with anything they could grab," Maureen projects onto these other people her own explosiveness. She craves order amidst the upheavals and restlessness of her world and when she finds it, she feels a compulsion to destroy the very order she sought.

Maureen's brother Jules is always bothered by that "something about life [which] he could not figure out." His futile attempts to bring order into his life, like his aching to set the salt and pepper shakers side by side during a family feud, underline his own need for even just the appearances of order: "they made sense together." But Jules is doomed never to achieve this order. Eventually he comes to the insight that life is mysterious, yet he still wonders why "the mystery was cast in the forms of such diminished people." Rather than seek tranquility as Maureen does, Jules seeks escape. First he escapes from his family, an action Maureen continually dreams of imitating; then later, he uses his car as the means of escaping from everything. "So long as he owned his own car he could always be in control of his fate—he was fated to nothing . . . His car was like a shell he could maneuver around, at impressive speeds; he was second generation to no one. He was his own ancestors" (*them* 356). His car is his means of transporting himself not only from the disorder of his life but also from history, from time, from lineage. If Maureen seeks a sense of history in the library, Jules seeks to be free of history in his car. The violent chaos of their lives drives them to seek even the most superficial semblance of order; salt and pepper shakers side by side and library books all neatly arranged. Through the juxtaposition of the images of order and those of disorder, Oates increases the tension of the narrative.

When Richard Everett in *Expensive People* visits the Fernwood Public Library with his mother, he is impressed with the "homey-home" quality of the building. As they enter the cozy, inviting library, they meet Mavis Grisell, and Nada sends a "sideways glance" to her son which assures him she would never leave him again. Nada has never cared for Mavis—who ironically is the woman Elwood marries after Nada's death. The purpose of this trip to the library has been for Nada to look up an article which praises her as a promising, young author. Charged with irony, the scene picks up the various themes of the novel: the homelike quality of the otherwise impersonal library exaggerates Richard's need for a home and for a mother. The irony implicit in the meeting of Richard's mother and soon-to-be stepmother, together with Nada's assurance that she would never leave again, mirrors the shallowness and superficiality of the relationships in the novel.

Richard explains his love for libraries, "all libraries, those sanctuaries for the maimed and undanceable, the lowly, pimply, neurotic, overweight, underweight, myopic, asthmatic . . . Few are the flirtations in a library, I insist, though Nada never had to search far for adventure. Few are the assaults, physical or verbal. Libraries exist for people like me" (EP 113). The technique of counterpointing the systematic order of the library with the chaotic disorder of the lives of the Everetts powerfully calls attention to the differences.

In addition to the images of the library and those of glassware and china is the equally powerful metaphor of consumption in *Expensive People*. Richard admits he is trying to kill himself by overeating, following the example of a relative. He has been tempted to stuff himself with money and die in that unique way, but he has not enough cash. Acquisition and consumption are all-important realities in the world of the Everetts. Devouring not only stuffed shrimp and lobster, "sinking into a slough of food," the expensive people consume one another and ultimately cost each other dearly. In their world, everything has a price tag, and the cost of living, for Richard, proves to be too high.

By means of the creation of various kinds of characters, from the gluttonous Max, who devours not only great quantities of food but also great numbers of people, through the child Richard Everett, who tries to satiate his hunger for love by eating, to the idealistic Jules who dreams of a new society, the refrain reverberates in Oates's fiction: people are fragile, easily hurt and destroyed, easily victimized. As he is wont to philosophize, Max warns Karen that " 'people are so delicate, a word misspoken might never be amended, a look of the wrong sort never negated . . .' " (WSF 184).

Using the image of a racetrack, Max also explains to Karen the order of the universe in terms of the laws of centrifugal and centripetal forces. There are " 'two pressures' " he elaborates, " 'one pushing in, the other pushing out. That's how our lives are. . . . the pressures are opposed, they fight each other. The law of the circle . . . two forces, one to live and one to die' " (WSF 140). Our lives are lived in the tension between the two forces; the universe is ordered by these opposing forces. Later, talking to her about *Paradise Lost,* " 'a long poem he had been rereading,' " Max takes pains to expound his belief that there is no paradise: " 'The only important thing is that we have no paradise: we have none' " (WSF 182). Any pulling force toward an outer world, a spiritual world is illusion. Consequently all questing for order and meaning is folly. We are trapped in a disordered world, which according to Max is the only world.

This image of entrapment is integrally linked to violence in the novel. Karen feels, when a fight erupts between her father and Shar, "once more a creature trapped within a dream, waiting for release. The unreal violence of the past few minutes rushed to a climax and exploded in her brain as she felt the impact of her father's disgust" (WSF 72). The double image of cloaking the very real violence as a dream and of awaiting release from a trap successfully carries forward the ironically muted violence of the scene. The need for freedom suggested by the image of entrapment recurs often in the novel. Shar clings to his freedom as Karen increasingly threatens to infringe on that freedom. She concludes that no one is really free: "If some men supposed themselves free it was only because they did not understand that they were imprisoned—bars could be made of any shadowy substance, any dreamy loss of light" (WSF 161). She has already surrendered her freedom by leaving her father and following Shar; she understands something he has not yet learned: there is no such thing as total freedom.

A suggestion of entrapment is further conveyed in the description of Karen's feeling that "they might have been two people condemned to an eternity in each other's presence, lovers or criminals who had sinned together on earth but who could not understand precisely what they had done, or why, or in what way it was a sin demanding damnation" (WSF 167). Trapped, condemned to each other by their very relationship with one another, they do not understand why they must be so punished. Fully aware of her destructive effect on Shar, Karen understands "his hatred for her as a token of their growing familiarity." Life has become so disordered that love destroys, reality becomes a dream, and one is trapped in this existence.

Some of the power to give a sense of order to reality comes from that same power of language to give some semblance of order or meaning to human experience. The ability to name something, to articulate and record, confers on the speaker some power or mastery over his world. Oates astutely comments on this power of language when, discussing Harriette Arnow's book *The Dollmaker*, she notes that we are called upon to complete the characters of that novel with words, to fill them out and to enflesh them with our own language. *The Dollmaker*, she writes, "deals with human beings to whom language is not a means of changing or even expressing reality, but a means of powerfully recording its effect upon the nerves."[6] Language grants some measure of control over one's fate; the ability to define and to record is the first step toward achieving that control.

Language is not only that power which elevates man above other living things, but it is also his only weapon against annihilation and destruction. Man re-creates the world through language, according to Oates. It is all he has "to pit against death and silence." Silence, she maintains, is the opposite of language and "silence for human beings is death."[7]

Implicit in Richard Everett's opening remarks in *Expensive People* is this belief in the power of language. Discussing his rejection of various beginnings of his novel, he writes: "If you have to begin your life with a sentence, better make it a brave summing up and not anything coy: *I was a child murderer*" (EP 6). The pun and the posed insouciance do not mollify the impact of the statement. Richard's action of writing his memoirs, which read like a compulsive confession, is an effort to come to terms with his own confused feelings. By attempting to give his disordered world the order which language confers, he tries to identify and sort out his love-hate feelings toward his parents. He speaks of seeking a language for his memoir and of turning "desperately to the works of 'culture'" and only finding the "same kind of seething, tortured products" as the one he is writing. Any order or beauty he finds is surface only, and he consoles himself with a quote from Tennyson—"'We poets are vessels to produce poetry and other excrement'" (EP 103)—which undercuts his very search for a language to give order and meaning to his art and by extension to his life.[8]

In *A Garden of Earthly Delights*, Lowry flees Clara because he cannot talk to her. Their relationship ends because they have run out of words to use with each other. The failure of language is responsible in large measure for the failure of their relationship; they need language to complete their love, and when they cannot find the words, when they do not have the power of language, they must separate. Lowry's son Swan realizes he has the same difficulty when he tries to talk to his girl friend, Loretta. "He did not know the style of language and behavior the other boys knew instinctively. He did not know what to say or do and the knowledge of his stupidity depressed him" (GED 399). He understands that he cannot talk to her, just as his father could not talk to Clara. The tragic inability to use language contributes to the destruction of both men.

On the other hand, Clara and Swan, in their conspiratorial relationship, achieve power over Revere by always referring to him as "he." They can maintain a distance and a noninvolvement through language. "Revere was *he* to Clara and Swan; it was an impersonal pronoun that always remained impersonal" (GED 358). Similarly, Swan assuages his conscience of any guilt in the shooting of Robert by thinking of the boy as " 'Robert.' " Although his responsibility in the death is never clearly established, he is haunted by the memory of the event, until through language, he can objectify the dead boy.

Torn between his love for his mother and his revulsion at her suspected promiscuity, Swan uses language to hurt her. When Clara deposits him at the library, the paradigm of order, while she carries on an affair in town, a word forces itself out of him: " 'That bitch.' " Calling her that name empowers him to punish her because "that name was a punishment, even if she did not know what he had done." When Revere's other son, Jonathan, calls her a " 'goddam filthy bitch' " to his friends, it is not directed at the same purpose. His use is simply descriptive; Swan's is punitive.

When Swan is finally called upon to use language, he cannot. After driving all night to the home where Clara and Revere live, he cannot explain why he had come. He can only stammer, " 'I want to ... ! I want to explain something to you' " (GED 438). But words fail him again, he feels as if his lips are swollen and "too large to move," so he resorts to physical language and picks up his gun. Still unable to speak he kills Revere and himself.

Part of Howard Wendall's failure as a human being is his similar failure to use language. The Wendall menage is described as a "tomb of a house of silent men," where only the youthful exuberance of the child Jules is heard because "Howard, gone off to war, was no more silent in his absence than he had been at home" (*them* 70). A "silent and angry man," Howard is powerless to use words in any way; he merely broods and lumbers about like a dumb animal. By contrast, Jules is fascinated with the power of language. As a very small child he believes words have a magic power, and at school his classmates are captivated by his "magic words." Once when he had witnessed a hideous plane crash in which a man's head had been sheared off " 'like with an ax,' " he had hidden himself in the family barn. When Loretta finds him, he is stammering, "the beginnings of words stumbling over themselves and piling up so that nothing could get loose, as if he were choking, so small a boy suffocating with the urgency to speak" (*them* 72). He senses, as young as he is, that to be able to speak about the horror he had seen would somehow enable him to cope with it better.

In *Do With Me What You Will*, Elena Ross cannot speak of her terrifying experience of being kidnapped and neglected by her father. Suffering from both the physical and psychological effects of such an ordeal, she cannot speak. When she tries to talk the words only go around in her head and will not come out of her mouth. She mentally describes the experience as: "*There were two streams of words: one in the head, where you can feel them like stones, hard little things, getting ready to be said out loud, and one in the throat and up into the back of the mouth and the mouth itself, on the tongue, and there the words are in the shape of air. Bubbles. The two streams of words come together in the back of your mouth, where you swallow, but sometimes they don't then people stare at you. Then they laugh.*" But the words in her head will neither come out nor will they dissolve. "*They hurt. Passing through the parts of the head they hurt, they swell up and get big. Words in the throat like crying, swallows of air. You swallow them by mistake*" (DWM 40). Like Jules, she instinctively realizes the power of language to help give order and meaning to even the most frightening of experiences, but she is powerless to speak. When she finally does talk, the ironic statement is made: "*And the world became perfect again.*" The world never was nor will it ever be perfect for Elena, but at least the power to speak enables her to come to some terms with her world.

Words are given shape in silence; in silence, too, a deeper communication can sometimes take place. Even the erratic and irresponsible relationship between Karen and Shar has its "periods of real silence that were more intimate than anything Karen had ever experienced" (WSF 172). She does not have to tell Shar that she will not consider having an abortion, her wordless response can have no other meaning. At other times, Karen uses her silence as a weapon against Shar. She encloses herself protectively in it, beyond his reach. Clara, too, realizes that it can be a protection; locked secretively in silence she knows "that way no one could get you" (GED 136). She runs from the revelatory power of words, just as Maureen recognizes that a "private language" can separate people. Without a common language there can be no communication, no use of the power of words.

Words may also violate a kind of sacred silence between two people as in *Wonderland*. When Jesse Harte comes to live with his grandfather after the tragic death of his family, the silence between the two has a healing effect on the boy. However, once the grandfather explodes in anger to Jesse, their silence becomes "dirtied by words." Jesse cannot understand how his grandfather can speak so, "how he could be putting [those things] into words?" Their "partnership of silence" has been violated. "It was not that his grandfather had said anything wrong, but that he had said anything at all," which perplexes Jesse most. Words have become a betrayal, and Jesse knows he can no longer live in the house of his relative.

Oates consistently imputes to language antithetical powers: one to heal and one to destroy. Consonant with her use of rhetorical violence, she frequently focuses the reader's attention on the latter. When verbal language fails, her characters fall back on physical language—beating and killing—or they retreat to silence. Throughout her works, however, is the underlying belief that language has some power, some potential to help man give order and meaning to his inchoate world, if he could but find and use the right words. Her fiction itself stands as testimony to this belief.

She repeatedly affirms her belief that the "customary use of language [is] to restore, with its magical eloquence, the lost humanity of the tragic figure . . ." (EOI 12). By enriching her narratives with rhetorical violence, she reenforces her understanding that violence often becomes a substitute for verbal language. Deaths, murders, killings in her fiction are often "only paradigms for a language of random destruction."[9] By her adroit use of such rhetorical devices as employing modifiers and verbals which connote violence and hostility, describing things and people in images of shattering glassware and trapped animals, giving her narratives a breathless pace, and, while acknowledging the ordering power of language, calling attention to its equally powerful ability to destroy, Joyce Carol Oates creates a language of violence and tragedy which infuses into her narratives an horrific ambiance of violence. Not only are the central episodes violent—rape, murder, suicide, riots, beatings—but the smallest descriptive details are also. The ultimate effect of this technique is the creation of fiction permeated with violence and tragedy. Oates's works offer nothing to mollify or diminish the intensity of her tragic vision.

FIVE

The tragic vision

If we had immortal life (but we don't), it'd be reasonable to do as we do now: spend our time killing one another ...

John Cage, "DIARY: How to Improve the World (You Will Only Make Matters Worse) Continued 1969 (Part V)" *Liberations*

1

One of Joyce Carol Oates's persistent concerns is to make the tragic vision real to the twentieth century. She seeks through her works to awaken contemporary society to its own destruction, to deepen the consciousness of her readers to the tragic dimensions of life. This task demands that her own perceptions of the times be sharply defined, that she confront—because resolution is impossible—the ambiguities of the day without trying to answer them, and that in so doing she offer to her readers something more than the sensationalism of the daily news.

From Oates's fiction—particularly those places where she indulges in authorial intrusion or philosophizing about art and writing—and from her essays, it is possible to cull a theory of art. She has stated often that art, particularly great art, is necessarily flawed—not because the artist's vision is inadequate, but because his vision is too adequate. The artist recognizes, as others before her noted, "Life is a mystery to be lived, not a problem to be solved." Life is a riddle: unsolvable but not inscrutable. Oates likens this paradox to a Zen koan which is an experience and not a puzzle. To solve the koan is to solve the vexing problem of existence itself (NHNE 267–68). It is to this relentless scrutiny that Oates addresses herself. Her theory of art might well be formulated: *human life is an inescapable tragedy which, unless and until it is so recognized, can never be transcended.* Her entire body of writings is thus directed at the recognition of this tragedy. In Oates's world the greatest mistake is not to succumb to the tragic but to fail to recognize it.

This tragic mystery of life cannot be solved, and it is futile to try, but it must be explored. Oates often refers to Franz Kafka to whom she has a certain indebtedness. Frequently a character will quote Kafka, as in the case of Sylvia, who reminds her estranged husband of his earlier fondness for two lines from Kafka's diaries, " 'What an effort to keep alive! Erecting a monument does not require the expenditure of so much strength' " (MI 123). Merely remaining alive is a victory. Where Kafka, however, does not believe in tragedy, Oates does. She is firmly rooted in the tradition of tragedy, in a belief in the self which struggles to achieve personality and identity and to transcend.

Without attempting the impossible—the formulation of a precise, simple, clear definition of tragedy—it is nevertheless possible to discuss the tragic dimensions of Oates's works as well as to describe the tragic vision which informs them. Certainly none of her characters are "tragic heroes" in the traditional or classical sense of the concept. Hers are the tragic tales of ordinary men and women who suffer, are exploited, and are destroyed, often without knowing it. Their significance lies only in their ability to survive, to "get through," to cope with the limitations of the human world. For

Oates, the subject matter of tragedy has always been this heroic, but failed, striving against inexorable powers.

Her narratives reveal the petty lives and struggles of unheroic human beings. Writing on the drama of the absurd, Oates expresses a fundamental difficulty with which she grapples in her writings: "how to create tragedy, which is predicated upon the uniqueness of human beings, in a leveled world in which all are equal and all are perhaps without value" (EOI 124). This dilemma persistently plagues her works. In the fictive world which she has created, her characters are all equal—all are victims. How much she posits value in them as human beings is difficult to say; certainly the characters recognize little value in one another, and society, as depicted in the novels, seems not genuinely to value human life generally nor the individual particularly. Where one expects to find sympathy and concern, one finds only rebuff and humiliation. In school, children are belittled and berated for their ignorance and illiteracy (GED 42–50, *them* 74). Social agencies are dehumanizing, as Grandma Wendall experiences when she visits the clinic in Detroit (*them* 103–7). The church women who call on the Walpoles are repulsed by what they see; Clara astutely observes the "strange discrepancy between their mouths, which were smiling, and their eyes, which looked frightened . . ." (GED 91). Not even Jack Morrissey's adolescent discovery of "superior people" (DWM 198) repudiates the fundamental equality, characteristic of Oates's "leveled" world.

Suffering and poverty—both economic and psychological—bring her characters to the same level and raise the issue of their personal value and worth. Oates's tragedies deal with ordinary people who are struggling to make sense of their lives and who work at defining themselves. It is they who endure the "ceaseless struggle with the fabric of the universe . . . a constant, daily heart-breaking struggle over money, waged against every other ant-like inhabitant of the city, the stakes indefinable beyond next month's payment of rent or payment on the car."[1]

Tragic literature deals with the deepest questions of human existence and the meaning of life, of the presence or possibility of order in the shaping of reality. To date, Joyce Carol Oates's major works have raised and wrestled with these questions. Oates knows—as we all do—that there are no final solutions; the important thing is to pursue the right questions and to continue the searching. All of her works are attempts to answer the question Maureen Wendall asks of her fictional teacher, Joyce Carol Oates: "How can I live my life if the world is like this?" (*them* 330). Because this is an imperfect world, because a feeling of impotence leads a person to violence, because the need for community is so frequently thwarted and unfulfilled, because this is a tragically diminished urban world, we all ask Maureen's question. The tragic vision which informs Oates's works reflects her perceptions of the twentieth century—and it yields the hope of a hope.

Oates repeatedly searches for the meaning and purpose of art. In her prefatory comments in *Scenes from American Life*, she identifies three types of art: "works of art that explain nothing that dispel order and sanity; works of art that contradict our experience . . . ; works of art that refuse to make sense. . . ."[2] But, art, for Oates, must be purposeful, born from an irresistible necessity to create, to transform, and to reveal. The interaction, the exchange between the artist together with his art and the personality who receives the art, is sacred. Nowhere does she write more strongly and emphatically about this relationship and the consequent responsibility of the artist than in *New Heaven and New Earth*. If art indeed can refuse to make sense, can explain nothing, can contradict experience, it must do so as an effort to illumine human experience and to give some shaping order to the terrifying tragedy of our time. "When exceptional individuals integrate the warring elements of our culture in themselves," she writes, "and experience in themselves the evidently 'tragic' personality of the epoch, we have great art." The "serious artist insists upon the sanctity of the world" and does not shrink from presenting his tragic vision in his art. He does so "to force up into consciousness the most perverse and terrifying possibilities of the epoch, so that they can be dealt with and not simply feared. . . ." Such is his mission as artist. He may be dismissed, or "denounced as vicious and disgusting," when in reality he is "in the service of [his] epoch" (NHNE 6, 7).

The artist then must in some way be immune to negative or un-favorable criticism because he creates out of an intense inner con-viction that his vision ought to be shared, and that it can affect another's perceptions. Oates repeatedly refutes the assumption that art should please. She questions whether we should even want to be pleased. "It is only through disruption and confusion that we grow," she contends, "jarred out of ourselves by the collision of someone else's private world [the artist's] with our own."[3]

Much of Oates's fiction has been criticized for being vicious or disgusting—but such negative reaction does not deter her from continuing to write out of her tragic vision, spurred on, no doubt by her own sense of what her responsibility as an artist is and of the power of art. She implicitly likens herself to Franz Kafka when she quotes in the epigraph to *New Heaven and New Earth*, "Evil does not exist; once you have crossed the threshold, all is good. Once in another world, you must hold your tongue."[4] After this, there can only be affirmation, an affirmation which yields to "only existence."

Only then does one hold one's tongue. But for Oates the visionary of our time cannot escape his mission to attempt to analyze and to record the tragedy of the epoch—even though his art may be "dis-turbing, vicious and disgusting." He must speak. "Such artists," she continues, "are passionate believers in the authenticity of their visions. . ." (NHNE 6).

The paradise / hell paradox only obfuscates the power of great art to reveal what is truly tragic, to awaken the consciousness of others to inexplicable mysteries of human life. Evil does exist in Oates's fictive world, personal evil and guilt, malevolent forces in the world which threaten to "unhinge the universe" (AF 46). It is Oates's firm conviction that that evil can and should be exorcised.

By continually focusing her works on small, miserable, and un-happy people, Oates forces her reader to examine these lives in de-tail, from every conceivable point of view. With the persistence of an air hammer she drives home her theme: that human life can be redeemed.

Oates's fiction is imbued with the "tragic sense of life" of which Miguel de Unamuno writes, a sense which "carries with it a whole conception of life itself and of the universe . . . [which] does not so much flow from ideas as determine them . . ."[5] Hers is a vision of both the sensible world and the ideal world, the "child of hunger" and the "child of love" of the Spanish philosopher.[6] Her fiction emphasizes most explicitly the world of hunger, yet it nevertheless yields the possibility of the ideal of love. With keen insight, she shares the tragic awareness of Unamuno that if "the problem of life, the problem of bread, were once solved, the earth would be turned into a hell by the emergence in a more violent form of the struggle for survival."[7] Once the tragic cycle has begun, there is no stopping it. The continuous and growing pressure to survive, to climb, to surpass metastasizes, killing off all other human aspirations and ambitions and tragically strangling any possibility of self-fulfillment and community.

The capstone of modern tragedy is the "lamentable loss of connection between men," according to Raymond Williams in his analysis of modern tragic literature.[8] Oates focuses not only on the loss itself but also on the effect it has on the person. Pushed to the furthest limits of human endurance, Oates's characters cling to the hope that so long as they can connect with someone else, so long as they can dial a number, they can live. Terrifying as this loss of connection is, there remains the undying hope of restoring a sense of connectedness.

While it is not the only profound and reasoned sense of life, the tragic vision is the "antithesis of popular vision, or lack of vision, in its comprehension of complexity, incongruity and paradox."[9] A tragic vision need not be despairing; though it cannot be naïvely optimistic, it can, in fact, be affirmative and celebrate life. The most profound tragedy reveals, according to Richard Sewall, "a full if fleeting vision, through the temporary disorder, of an ordered universe." Sewall goes on to explore the essence of that tragic vision, which is

in its first phase primal, or primitive, in that it calls up out of the depths the first (and the last) of all questions, the question of existence: What does it mean to be. It recalls the original terror, harking back to a world that antedates the conceptions of philosophy, the consolations of later religions, and whatever constructions the human mind has devised to persuade itself that the universe is secure. It recalls the original un-reason, the terror of the irrational. It sees man as questioner, naked, unaccommodated, alone, facing the mysterious, demonic forces in his own nature and outside, and the irreducible facts of suffering and death. Thus it is not for those who cannot live with unsolved questions and unresolved doubts, whose bent of mind would reduce the fact of evil into something else or resolve it into some larger whole.[10]

It is man, the unaccommodated, lonely searcher who is at the heart of Oates's tragedies: man asking if the world is like this, how he can live his life.

In the face of what is "questionable and terrible," the "tragic artist is no pessimist—he says *yea* to everything,"[11] according to Friedrich Nietzsche. This close affinity between the tragic vision and affirmation is emphatically reiterated in Nietzsche's essays, as it is persuasively demonstrated in Oates's fiction. The philosopher promises the "advent of a tragic age, during [which will flower] the highest art in the saying of yea to life, 'tragedy' . . ."[12] Consequently, to the tragic artist, the question of how man can live in this world never implies the alternative of not living but seeks to know the manner in which he may survive and one day transcend.

Sewall observes that no civilization, no matter how advanced or superior a culture it enjoys, is immune from this questioning. The original terror may return at any time, and the old formulations cannot dispel it. There is never a time impervious to the sudden jarring loose again of the questions of human destiny and ultimate justice.[13] The tragic vision must necessarily be tailored to the historical and existential situation, but its essence is unchanging. Man returns again and again to the same questions of the meaning and purpose of the universe and of his individual existence.

A tragic vision is incisive; it cuts through to the very life. Without resolving the ambiguities of life, without minimizing the pain, it offers a vision of man—alone and lonely, struggling both to be free and to be himself, bent on creating his world. It does not shrink from the harsh reality of the human situation, but it searches out the contours and dimensions of that reality to discover its meaning, its order. The tragic vision is a testimony to the fact that man spends a good part of his life waiting, "thinking, remembering, dreaming, waiting for something to come ... and give a shape to so much pain" (*them* 341). The man with tragic vision has an "attitude of attentiveness to the contingencies and sufferings that it is the lot of man to endure," and he is "engaged by a dream of some brave new world or country of the spirit wherein the brokenness of man may be repaired and healed."[14]

Any complete vision of the tragic must necessarily face the problem of evil. It must not, as Sewall warns, magnify evil into something greater than it really is, nor can it reduce it to something else. Evil in Joyce Carol Oates's world is that tragically created by human beings. It is born out of feelings of self-worthlessness, of powerlessness, of hatred, of selfishness. Not an impersonal, malevolent force, evil is rather created by characters often incapable of fully realizing what it is they are doing.[15] It may be the product of blind emotion, but it is always the creation of man. The focus of Oates's novels, however, is on the social effects or consequences of evil—from Karen Herz's willful complicity in the death of Shar Rule through Elena Howe's skillful manipulation of Jack Morrissey away from his wife and their adopted child. The emphasis is not on what prompts or motivates the evil but on the effect it has on the lives of others.

Oates does not search out the root of evil in the human heart. Her novels deal with the surfaces of the lives of her characters, because that is all they can comprehend. Only the occasional glimpses she gives of the corrosive sense of impotence suggest a possible source of evil. Nowhere does she analyze those drives and forces within man that lead him to execute evil. The evil on which she focuses the attention of her novels is the evil of society, and since society is man, it is the evil of man's own making. Her novels depict evil; they do not try to discover its causes.

Of central concern in her tragic vision is the destruction of simple people and the sad fact of their not realizing and consequently of their not being able to resist this destruction. What most frequently destroys them is, tragically, their own lack of self-identity and self-fulfillment. When she discusses the thesis of Wendell Berry's "A Place on Earth," Oates comes close to articulating the thrust behind all her works. "The earth and human relationships are our only hope," she muses. But "to be 'saved' in this culture one must sell oneself as shrewdly as possible. One's fate depends not upon his sacred relationship with the land, but his secular deceptive relationship with society."[16] Something is wrong, deeply wrong: the simple and the poor suffer the most because in their simplicity they fail to see their destruction, and in their poverty, they are powerless, even if they could see, to change radically the way things are.

But Oates is committed in her fiction to the raising of the consciousness of those who are being destroyed. Her writings are part of her attempt to awaken in them an awareness of the tragic dimensions of their lives. She promises, moreover, to move from an extreme concentration on the nightmare quality of modern life to a more optimistic, affirmative stance. Through her writings, she hopes, eventually, to offer a vision of transcendence. More than merely "getting through," more than just holding together the thousand pieces of one's life, her promised vision will point the way, for those who possess a tragic vision, toward finding a shape for so much pain.

The tragic vision that informs and quickens Oates's fiction eschews simple answers and glib solutions. It is hard, unflinching, and at times, incredible. But as she explains in the introduction to *them*, she intends to deal with a fiction that seemingly cannot be real. But ultimately it is the "only kind of fiction that is real." In fact, she admits she has understated some of the facts because she feared "that too much reality would become unbearable."

Confronted with their tragic lot in life, Oates's characters flirt with a metaphysic of luck. Having long ago realized their impotence to change their fate, they surrender to it, reserving only the faint hope that one day their luck might change. The power of this hope in luck is nowhere more poignantly dramatized than in the gesture of Loretta, who, fleeing the scene of the murder of her young lover, stops to pick up a penny for good luck (*them* 41). When it would appear that nothing worse could possibly happen, at least one can simply or naïvely hope that one's luck might change. Without this kind of optimism, it might not be possible to survive at all. Loretta figuratively picks up pennies for "good luck" throughout her life, for had she not this simple hope, she could not go on. Although Oates herself condemns a facile optimism, she at the same time acquiesces in the belief that survival is possible only for those who do hope. Literature is "wonderfully optimistic," she hyperbolically exclaims in an interview, "because it so often demonstrates how human beings get through things, maneuver themselves through chaos, and then *write about it*."[17] Oates is consistent and successful in portraying the lives of little people who, when confronted with the almost overwhelming demands of life, tentatively attach their hopes to a dream of "better luck."

Because of this hope, nihilism has no place in Oates's fictive world. "Nothing can come from nothing," she affirms; "nihilism is overcome by the breaking-down of the dikes between human beings, the flowing of passion . . ." (EOI 6). In commenting on Herman Melville's *The Confidence Man*, she maintains that the "disintegration into nihilism must be resisted." Man is delicately poised between confidence and despair, "between the illusory contentment of charity and the confrontation of truth that will not be comforted— that is, despair" (EOI 80). Although it has often been regarded as a critical deficiency in Oates's writings, her characters rarely despair. They may have nervous breakdowns, they may withdraw into silence, they may escape by drinking or by running away—but not one of the central characters of her major works, no matter how extreme his straits may be, despairs. This may be a fault or weakness in the works, but it is nevertheless consistent with Oates's strong belief that not only survival, but also transcendence, is possible. She denounces those works of literature in which death is the way of transcendence. In her own writings, this stance, directly opposed to nihilism, is easily discernible, although at times it is also less than convincing. Writing of Eugene Ionesco's art, she laments that it is the "tragic expression of those who cannot transcend the crippling biological, social, and accidental banality of their lives. The only 'transcending' is death, but this is surely a parody of what man has always meant by the transcending of his mortal life" (EOI 227). Firm and inflexible is her belief in the power of human beings to endure; intolerant is she of those artists whose vision is nihilistic and nonaffirming.

Never, however, in all her fiction does Oates reveal what inner power or strength enables her characters to get through. We see only persons buffeted and beset by the most unspeakable trials and sufferings and successfully maneuvering themselves through the chaos. But the vexing question remains: what enabled them to endure? We see them only from the outside, and while we may applaud their endurance, we are nevertheless perplexed by not knowing how they accomplished it.

A definite evolution is discernible in the characters from *With Shuddering Fall* to *Do With Me What You Will*. For the persons in the early novels, life is an accident, events happen wantonly and randomly. The characters who emerge in the later fiction have a tendency to be more resolute, more determined to take life into their hands, and more capable of coming to terms with their destiny. If there is one consistent refrain in Oates's six novels, it is "I must take control of my life." Feebly enunciated at first by the characters of the early novels, it grows stronger and clearer in those of the later works.

Carleton in *A Garden of Earthly Delights* sums up the attitude toward life among the early characters when he reflects on the accident which opens the novel. One is destined for a certain number of accidents in his life and the sooner they take place, the better. Although this collision is untimely, he is glad that there is one less accident in store for him now. This impoverished logic characterizes the general feeling toward fate and destiny among the people of Oates's early works. Life has certain things in store for one: these things are inevitable and inescapable. The appropriate posture is one of waiting for them to happen.

In Carleton's world, one can "predict nothing" and "nothing is the way it should be." The tragedy of Carleton's life is that he feels he has no power to do anything about the way things are. Things happen to him and he dumbly lets them occur. Clara has this same resigned—almost supine—posture toward life. She believes "you can never count on nothing"; things happen or do not happen, they fall together or fall apart, and one can do nothing about it. One might wish things would be different, but there is no way to change them. For Clara the world is controlled by others and one has to give in, in all that does not matter. Seemingly, she has no awareness of her own ability to take her life into her hands.

As Lowry entreats Clara to come away with him, he explains his frustration and inability to understand things because " 'nothing stays still long enough for you to understand it.' " Clara can so identify with this attitude that if she did not have responsibility for her child Swan she would run away with Lowry. What she admires most in him is his power, what she perceives as his knowing what he is doing. Pathetically, all Clara and later Swan want to do is to "get things straight. Put things in order." But they can see no way to accomplish this and consequently spend their lives passively letting things happen to them.

By the time she creates the characters of her later fiction, the Wendalls and particularly Jesse Vogel, Oates has moved to a somewhat more self-determining, less fatalistic character. Although Jules frequently laments that he is his fate (*them* 296), he has some awareness of his own role in his destiny. Maureen may be "doomed to be herself" (*them* 407), yet she recognizes that she has some part to play in that dooming. As a young boy, through Dr. Pederson's tutelage, Jesse learns that he must "*be what he was meant to be*" (W 73). Later, when he is more mature, he comes to the knowledge that he can and does "invent himself." The role of destiny, of fate, is never entirely dismissed; there is a remnant in even Oates's more fully developed characters, but it is no longer an omnipotent force in their lives; there is some sense of personal responsibility for one's destiny.

Intimately bound up with the issue of fate and destiny is that of order and meaning in the universe. Karen Herz voices the dilemma that besets those who search for order in this chaotic world. Beleaguered by her own mistakes, her selfishness and stubborn pride, she admits it is "insane to look for order in life and it is insane not to" (WSF 315). Not to search is as futile as to expect to find order through one's search. The mystery remains: the hope of finding order cannot be denied. "The total vision," Sewall writes, "is neither of doom nor redemption, but of something tantalizingly, precariously in between. We have no hope, yet we hope. It is tragic."[18]

The impetus for this hope is derived from the fact that we are all dreamers. Oates acknowledges from the start that we seek an absolute dream: a dream we admit is unattainable even as we indulge in it. Despite the incredible horrors they have to endure, most of Oates's central characters are dreamers. Jules, still looking for the unmapped Golden West, sets off for Los Angeles, fanning the fires of his dreams of a new society. Maureen moves to Dearborn, hoping at last to be safe. Loretta, about to be married for the third time, cherishes the renewed hope of happiness. As she chooses to leave Marvin Howe for Jack Morrissey, Elena sallies forth with the dream that she has found some secure peace in her life. The "crudity" of this absolute dream, Oates writes, "is redeemed by the beauty that so often surrounds this dream. One can explain the dream but never its beauty" (EOI 4). The existence of the absolute dream and its power to the dreamer are irrefutable and inexplicable. What the dream proffers is indefinable, immaterial, ephemeral, some vague expectation.

It is perhaps this vague dream which keeps Oates's characters going. Because the dream is never more clearly defined, we are left to imagine what it is they dream of and hope and wait for. Although the process—the hungering, the waiting, the dreaming—is very real, it is the object of their expectations that eludes us. We can identify with the hunger and dreams of the tragic hero. "The

[129]

hero dies into our imaginations as we, helplessly, live out lives that are never works of art—even the helpless lives of 'artists'!—and are never understood. Suffering is articulated in tragic literature, and so this literature is irresistible, a therapy of the soul" (EOI 4). The true context of a great work of art, Oates maintains, is "not history, but dreams," and since we all seek absolute dreams, we can identify with those of our tragic heroes. The dream is necessary if we are to escape or transcend this diminished, nightmare world.

Outlining the origin of tragic literature, Richard Sewall identifies three stages of development. At the first phase, early man recognized only the emotional level, the pain and the fear. From this he graduated to conceptualizing his suffering; he began to be able to contemplate and to spiritualize his feelings. When he proceeded to the third level, he was able to verbalize his sufferings and his pain, a development which provided for the birth of tragic literature.[19] In many ways, Oates recapitulates this evolution in her fiction. By far the majority of her characters are capable of experiencing only on the first level, of feeling the pain, the fear, the suffering. They experience the terror of not being able to explain or to conceptualize what is happening to them. Only a few of her more fully developed characters move to the second phase and are able to reflect on and contemplate their experiences. None of her characters are able to verbalize adequately their suffering. With the power of language denied them and faced with the resulting frustration, they revert to a primitive language of gesture and action, to the physical language of violence. They lash out against the suffering, trying to flail and subdue it.

Oates is very much concerned with the question of the presence or possibility of tragedy in this age. While she acknowledges the provocative theses of Joseph Wood Krutch, George Steiner, and Leon Abel, who argue the death of tragedy and the impossibility of tragedy in the Western world, she quietly continues to speak of modern tragedies and to search for viable forms of tragic literature in the twentieth century.

Acknowledging that a traditional concept of tragedy, a concept which required a God, is dead, Oates presses on toward a new basis of tragedy. "The art of tragedy," she writes, "grows out of a break between self and community, a sense of isolation" (EOI 3). Her search for new forms for tragic literature leads her to ask what tragedy has been dealing with all along, to which she responds, "has it not been the limitations of the human world? . . . If communal belief in God has diminished so that, as writers, we can no longer presume upon it, then a redefinition of God in terms of the furthest reaches of man's hallucinations can provide us with a new basis for tragedy. The abyss will always open for us, though it begins as a pencil mark, the parody of a crack; the shapes of human beasts—centaurs and satyrs and their remarkable companions—will always be returning with nostalgia to our great cities" (EOI 8). Modern tragedy is thus shaped by the dissolution of community, the death of God, and the transformation of the domestic landscape into wilderness.

Tragic literature is in some elusive way related to the effort of forging communal bonds. The power of an extraordinary work of literature lies "in its insistence on the barrenness of life, even a life lived in intimacy with other human beings, bound together by ties of real love and suffering."[20] If tragedy grows out of the failure to establish community, it must necessarily touch on the fundamental urge of men to become related to one another through the bonds of community. "Suffering," she notes, "does not draw us into brotherhood." And tragedy which, according to William Butler Yeats, seems to tear down the " 'dykes that separate man from man,' " Oates sees as an "aesthetic rather than humanistic" experience (EOI 156).[21] Tragedy, for Joyce Carol Oates, is in part an expression of the failure to answer the inexorable need to create community.

Because modern tragedy is contingent on the death of God, Oates has divorced herself from any notion of a godly universe. Evident in some of her early works is this struggle to purge herself, through her literature, of any remnant of belief.[22] The few allusions to religion, church, or God in her fiction seem to reflect her own growing aversion to religious belief. Karen Herz's "conversion" and repentence during the ceremony of the Mass in *With Shudder-*

ing Fall is hardly tenable. The comic depiction of the women who represent the local church in *A Garden of Earthly Delights* is a prelude to the grotesque religious service to which they invite Clara. Money becomes a deity in the lives of the expensive people, and the Wendall children look at lucre as their deliverance and salvation. Ardis once asks Elena if she believes in God, and the ensuing conversation reveals an interesting position on belief.

> ". . . Elena, do you believe in God? Do they teach you about God in school?"
> "No."
> "Well, do you believe in God?"
> Elena hesitated. "I don't know. . . . Do you believe in God?"
> "If I did, what then?"
> Elena laughed. "Then I might believe too."
> "Well, relax. I don't happen to believe in God or in anything." She raised her coffee cup slowly, thoughtfully, staring at Elena. "I believe in luck. Good and bad luck. That's a way of saying I don't believe in anything, isn't it?"
> "Maybe," Elena said cautiously.
> "I believe life is experimental," Ardis said. "Each person experimenting to see how far he can get. . ." (DWM 71)

From the first to the sixth novel, there is a gradual change in the attitudes of Oates's characters toward a concept of God—from angry, hostile rejection to complacent disregard, from fierce denial to casual nonchalance. Without a belief in God, the traditional basis for tragedy, one believes in luck, which is to say one does not believe in anything. But ironically one is forced, according to Oates, to conjure up a new definition of God which in turn provides the basis for a new kind of tragedy.

In her pursuit of tragedy, Oates creates works which are not cathartic. They contain none of the satisfaction or purgation that has traditionally been associated with tragedy. Modern tragedy, by her own definition, does not embrace catharsis, but "deepens our own sense of the mystery and sanctity of the human predicament."[23] Extraordinary works of literature, she emphasizes, are depressing; they do not elevate the spirit or purge the emotions. In this, she is quite consistent in her own writings. She stops before catharsis and the effect is shock, not relief or release. Some of the narratives do not really end, she merely stops telling them. Like the life which they reflect, they often do not arrive at a point of satisfactory denouement. Resolution in such works is denied.

Two of her works have been highly criticized for their inconclusive endings, *Wonderland* and *Do With Me What You Will*. There are two endings for *Wonderland*. After the publication of the hard-cover edition, Oates, under some pressure from the less than enthusiastic reviews, revised the ending for the paperbound edition. She explains that she resisted her intuition regarding the conclusion and then "in deepest humility" revised it: "a mistake that will never be repeated."[24] Readers have also not been entirely satisfied with the conclusion of *Do With Me What You Will*, calling it too ambiguous.[25] There is inadequate preparation for Elena and Jack's decision to run off together; the action is not entirely consistent with their characters as they have been developed. *them*, in many ways Oates's finest work, ends on the sad note of separation: Jules takes leave of Maureen—he is headed West and she is living in the dream that she can be happy and safe with Jim and the child she is pregnant with. The tale stops but is hardly concluded, and there certainly is no catharsis.

If this tragic literature offers no catharsis to its readers, there is even less relief available to the actors of the drama. Waiting for that which will give shape to their pain, Oates's characters frequently wonder how life itself is lived. Does the living come first and then the inventing, or is it the other way around? Is life invented first and then lived? This dilemma of literature-as-life and life-as-invention bewilders characters such as Jules and Elena. Jules actually thinks he is a fiction. "He thought of himself as a character in a book being written by himself, a fictional fifteen-year-old with the capacity to become anything, because he was fiction. What couldn't he make of himself?" (*them* 108). In a rare instance of authorial intrusion, Oates returns to this theme of life as fiction-making. She writes: "Like all lives, Jules's was long and richly tedious, vexed with prodigious details of physical existence he would have been ashamed to record, were he writing his own story; his story would deal with the spirit exclusively. He thought of himself as pure spirit struggling to break free of the morass of the flesh. . . . Of the effort the spirit makes, this is the subject of Jules's story; of its effort to achieve freedom, its breaking out into beauty, in patches of beauty perhaps anyway, and of Jules as an American youth—these are some of the struggles he would have thought worth recording" (*them* 274). In his struggle to define himself, Jules wonders if there is a script he should be reading or if he himself is writing that script. When he believes the latter, he has a feeling of power and control over his life. When he believes the former, he becomes the victim of his own tragic fate, struggling to make some sense out of his life.

Following one of her futile efforts to contact her mother after Ardis had arranged for Elena to marry Marvin Howe, Elena wants to ask her mother *"is life lived out to add up to a story, or is the story invented first so it can be lived out?"* (DWM 325). Elena puzzles this out to no conclusion. If there were a story for her life, she has not yet found it; if she were inventing it, she clearly is in a quandary about where to take it.

Whether it be the question of inventing the story of one's life, of awaiting the accidents life has in store, or of picking up pennies for good luck, a tragic vision informs all of the writings of Joyce Carol Oates. Each of her six novels in its own way harkens back to the haunting question of Maureen Wendall, a question that reaches back into time and history and dreams: how does one live one's life in a world like this?

2

Critical evaluation of the writings of Joyce Carol Oates runs the gamut from extraordinarily high praise to scathing indictment. Poised between these extremes awaiting evaluation lies the phenomenal body of works by this remarkable young woman author who adamantly insists that the novel as genre is not only not dead but that its "moral, educative, illustrative" power has not diminished. She avers that her future works will not focus so obsessively on this nightmarish world but will move to a more transcendent vision. Whether she can achieve this or not, only time will tell.

Time, too, will be the judge of her critical position in twentieth-century literature. Alfred Kazin insists she is caught in the avalanche of time, producing works not ambitious enough. He goes so far as to say that some of her works seem to be written to rid her mind of those characters who haunt it, and she has not created works that will live.[26] On the other hand, Calvin Bedient calls her one of the most formidable talents of the age.[27] Whatever judgment history will finally make on Joyce Carol Oates, she is an author who will have to be reckoned with.

Oates has been repeatedly questioned and often criticized on account of her productivity. In an average year she may bring into print a major novel, a couple of collections of short stories—some new, many previously published and reworked—a play, and numerous essays and criticism. Perhaps one explanation for the magnitude of her publications is her fear of silence, her almost obsessive concern to re-create the world through her art, her fear of not speaking to a generation in need of words to heal, to quicken to new life, to awaken.

There is an unsettling suspicion among critics that to write so much, so quickly, necessarily diminishes the quality of one's writing and tends to overwork certain themes. And to some extent this criticism, when applied to Oates, is valid: there is an unevenness, a spottiness about the quality of her works and an acknowledged repetitiveness of some themes.

This repetitiveness is puzzling as it gives rise to the question of irony and the criticism of lack of imagination. Does saying the same thing over and over again render the thematic concern ironic? Or does it reenforce it? In the case of Oates, it is difficult to argue for irony; the body of works she has produced to date cannot sustain the argument that she is ironic. She is far too insistent—and consistently insistent—not only in her fiction but in her essays and

[135]

criticism as well—on the primacy of art to reveal and sanctify the tragedy inherent in human life "by honoring its complexities."[28] She seems to have taken upon herself the mission to bring to the attention of her readers her own tragic vision. And she does so over and over again. Why? That is difficult to answer. Perhaps she feels that we, her readers, have not heard her, so she says it again in a different way. Perhaps she feels that she, as author, has not explored the myriad implications of her vision, and she chooses to continue the search. At any rate, she makes no apologies for the repetition; the clearest change in her fiction over the years has been her movement away from despair and toward optimism. Her new collection of short fiction concludes with the statement, "I was born" (G 468), one of the more affirmative endings found in her recent fiction. The basic thematic concern, however, remains unchanged.

In many ways in terms of style Oates is more a nineteenth-century novelist than one truly at home in the twentieth century. Her themes, of course, are contemporary, but her attention to detail, the density of her realism, and the straightforwardness of her narrative line are more akin to her nineteenth-century ancestors— James, Wharton, Howells, than to her twentieth-century contemporaries—Vonnegut, Fowles, Barth, Borges. Stylistically, Oates is not an innovator. Her fiction is grounded in the reality of everyday life, of small, often mean and wrong-headed victims. She creates no great tragic heroes—not even Mr. Sammler's or Maggie's—only children growing up in disjointed and fractured worlds; women hating their husbands only a little more than they hate themselves; men betraying their women and themselves.

Oates's fiction consistently raises the question of the meaning of human life. Although not always the conviction of her characters, there is an a priori acceptance in her writings that life has meaning. The final failure is not to fall prey to a bullet, not even to suffer a nervous breakdown, but it is to fail to find the meaning of one's existence: this is ultimate failure. All other, lesser failures pale in the face of this lack, and it is to this consciousness that most of her writing is directed. If there is one overriding concern throughout

[136]

her works, it is this: to bring to the awareness of her readers her belief that life, however chaotic and tragic, yields a meaning finally not only to be perceived but to be embraced.

The novel, she contends "is the most human of all art forms—there are truths we can get nowhere else but in the novel. . . ."[29] So it is to the novel that she continually turns to find a vehicle for the "truths" she wishes to reveal. She tends not to be experimental; her sole piece of satire, *Expensive People*, stands out as somewhat unsuccessful and unsatisfying compared with her later works. Her poetry is likewise not as good as her fiction. More often than not her poems read like abstracts of her fictional statements. She often composes in this fashion, putting her ideas into poetry first, then into short fiction, and, possibly, finally into novel form.

Her poem "You / Your" from *Love and Its Derangements* is a statement from another point of view of the tension and intensity of a search for identity and independence. The "You" of the poem is Jules, one of the central characters of *them*, the "your" is Nadine, his one-time mistress. The poem speaks of Nadine's achieving her identity from loving Jules, of her experience of being drawn "up to / 1 day," to the day of self-definition. Moreover, "if [he] were to turn her lightly / inside out / [she] would become the fixed center / of the famous universe."[30] How unlike the fictional rendering of the event in which Jules desperately needs Nadine to find himself. The poem, however, lacks the intensity—and the poignancy—of the fiction. A longer poem, "Lines For Those to Whom Tragedy Is Denied," from *Anonymous Sins and Other Poems*, depicts the lives of unhappy women—the heartbreak, the poverty, the unwanted pregnancies, the social climbing, the divorce, and the emptiness—themes one finds repeated in the fiction. As an art form, however, fiction is more available to Oates's audience. It is also the medium she most successfully speaks through.

Literature has always been a sensitive, responsive medium, creating and reflecting the attitudes and values of society. There can be no doubt about Oates's works reflecting contemporary society; they are masterpieces of that reflective attribute of literature. However, their thrust towards and their efficacy in creating values is somewhat more difficult to affirm. Despite the author's insistence on this fact, her art to date seemingly places undue weight on merely getting through, enduring the struggles of human existence, and barely, just barely, escaping the imminent danger of breaking into a million jagged jigsaw pieces. Somehow, while this yields the hope of final affirmation and celebration, it does not readily or staunchly posit a value in life itself, nor in the person who struggles.

Oates has been accused of being narrow and derivative, of producing bulk, popular fiction. And, at first glance, there seems to be some basis for this kind of critical comment. The appearance of five major novels in little more than as many years invites the observation of too much, too soon. But Oates's obvious growth as a novelist from *With Shuddering Fall* to *Do With Me What You Will* refutes this initial reaction. Her development as a prose stylist is clear: *A Garden of Earthly Delights*, as well as her earliest novel, *With Shuddering Fall*, represent what might well be considered an apprenticeship. *them* is without doubt her most successful novel; it is unsurpassed among her other works in the handling of character portrayal and in the achievement of style.

In reality much of Oates's fiction has a common tone and similar themes; works seem repetitious and extend into each other as slight variations of the same almost obsessive concerns. Within this organic body of writings is a turning from terror toward the direction of transcendence. The conclusions of her recent publications are more affirmative: Elena Howe leaves her husband; a young woman returns from the brink of death, "I was born"; Titus Skinner lights up the light bulb.

With her last novels, Oates is beginning to experiment more freely in the actual narration of her tales. She departs from the straightforward, chronological approach she had successfully employed in *them*, *Wonderland*, and *A Garden of Earthly Delights* toward a more loose, sometimes stream of consciousness, sometimes surrealistic narration in *Expensive People* and *Do With Me What You Will*. So far this kind of experimentation has been tentative and somewhat timorous, often interjected between segments of chronological development, and often not entirely integrated into

[138]

the text. She is more freely and successfully experimental in her short stories, where without question, she is a contemporary master.

In those of her works which explore the search for one's personality, Oates often sounds Borgesian. In fact, *Wonderland* contains an epigraph from *Labyrinths* which speaks to the concern of this quest. Where Jorge Luis Borges deals with abstractions of this theme, Oates vividly attempts to re-create the nightmarish reality of waking to find one is only a dream—a protoplasm searching for a personality. For Oates the tragic dimensions of individual human life are not the larger issues of being or truth or goodness but the immensely exaggerated struggle to find meaning in toothaches and ants in sugar bowls. She writes of a typical character: "Never had a corner of her mind resisted the illumination of knowledge, any kind of knowledge: nothing had ever seemed to her too sordid to be true. Gradually all things—her father's drunkenness, her first husband's cowlike weakness, the cancer that had killed her mother, the drought that plagued everyone in late summer, the bitterness of winter, ants in sugar bowls, toothaches, the long lethargy of having a baby, the finality of the grave that overtook everyone in time—all—blurred as if they were no more than water in water, everything blended to the same texture, so that Anna never condemned anything that was " 'the way life is' " (G 58). The petty problems of daily life erode and threaten to shatter the fragile hold one has on the meaning of his existence. But he doesn't stop to examine these things, they are life as it is—unquestioned because questioning could reveal the emptiness, unexamined because one does not have the insight to examine, unconquered because conquest demands power. The honored complexities of Oates's fictional world are often nothing more than ants in the sugar bowls.

The haunting question returns: how can it be lived? how can this life be lived? One can live it in mindless resignation of its futility or one can live it in endless searching for its meaning. Many Oates characters adopt the former posture: life can only be endured when one accepts the tilting floor and the ants. "A thought rises shrilly in / someone's mind." Oates writes in "A Rising and Sinking and Rising in My Mind," "you cannot / change your life, or anything" (AS 64). This resignation, this acceptance makes life livable—for most of Oates's characters.

There are a few, however, who seek to be reborn, who, despite the pain involved, struggle to establish their identities and seek to maintain their footing on the tilting floor. Many of Oates's characters live with the apprehension that "a careless move will unhinge / the universe" (AF 46). A noted deficiency of Oates's fiction seems to be the complete absence of any character who has been reborn or who has succeeded in however small a way to take hold of his life. Without this, the focus of her writings remains steadily on the struggle—despite her promise to move to a more optimistic and affirmative posture.

With the exception of *Do With Me What You Will*, her novels are not carefully plotted; they are reflections of life—random, haphazard, and unpredictable. *Do With Me What You Will* is more artfully controlled. Oates sustains strong narrative interest by telling Elena's history in the first part, Jack's in the second, bringing the two characters together at the end of part two, then in her third segment unfolding the story of their relationship. This is an interesting deviation from the earlier novels and may indicate a breakthrough in her prose style.

Oates's works are limited, and she pays a price for her lack of humor. The tragic burden of the lives of her characters at times becomes barely tolerable and excessively oppressive: unrelieved, catastrophic events strain, if not defy, the imagination. Oates's characters may be ordinary people in one sense, but they suffer an extraordinary number of misfortunes and endure unbelievable afflictions—factors which tend to limit the works.

Unless she can move away from the two-dimensional, often superficial characters to which she has thus far almost solely confined herself and more directly towards her announced stronger moral posture and affirmative, transcendent vision, Oates will be doomed to repeating herself—a criticism frequently leveled at her at present. She has richly exploited the resources of her thematic concerns and of her choice of characters, and unless she moves on, she will become derivative of herself. Her tragically diminished people have told their tales, and their power to raise our consciousness is fast becoming exhausted. Her response to the complex phenomenon of urban life amounts to a deeply sensitive witness, but unless she is able to go beyond this, she fates herself to monotony and redundancy.

In addition to her concern with the tragic dimensions of modern life, Oates's fiction reveals her interest in the perennial questions of the relation of art to life and of the creation-invention of personality. Evidence of these interests is available in her criticism as well as her fiction. Because her writings on personality are tentative and germinal, it is difficult to define her theory and impossible to suggest its ultimate effect on her works. On the other hand, the art-life question is firmly established and answered in her writings.

When Maureen Wendall asks her fictional teacher, Joyce Carol Oates, to explain the value of literature, we never learn, in the context of the novel, the teacher's response. Maureen asks her how the books—"mainly lies"—which she taught in her class could possibly relate to the world outside, the world of "tanks and soldiers, people lying in the street" (*them* 329). How could Madame Bovary be important to the life of Maureen Wendall. *them*, itself, is a partial answer to the student's queries: *them* does have tanks and guns and people dying in the streets, it is filled with the "jumble" of life. More explicitly, however, Oates answers Maureen's questions in her essay "Art: Therapy and Magic" in which she writes: "The experience of reading a great novel (*Madame Bovary*, for instance) is the experience of having lived through and transcended the limits of that world, *even* the limits of that aesthetic world."[31] Literature empowers us to see beyond the present, beyond the existential and aesthetic world, to the absolute dream. But the ability to see beyond is predicated on the prior ability to see, clearly, thoroughly, and tragically, the present. It is to the authentic and unadulterated presentation of this tragic vision of the now that Joyce Carol Oates is committed.

Notes

Chapter one (*pages 3–30*)

1. Joyce Carol Oates, "Remarks by Joyce Carol Oates Accepting the National Book Award for 'them,' " press release, Vanguard Press, March 4, 1970, p. 1. (See Appendix A.)
2. Walter Clemons, "Joyce Carol Oates: Love and Violence," *Newsweek*, 11 Dec. 1972, p. 77.
3. Joyce Carol Oates, "A Visit with Doris Lessing," *Southern Review*, 9 (Oct. 1973): 881.
4. Oates, "Remarks," p. 2.
5. "Transformations of Self: An Interview with Joyce Carol Oates," *Ohio Review*, 15 (Fall 1973): 53, 58. See also Clemons, p. 77.
6. Joyce Carol Oates, "An American Tragedy," *New York Times Book Review*, 24 Jan. 1971, p. 2.
7. "Transformations of Self," p. 53.
8. David Goldknopf, *The Life of the Novel* (Chicago: University of Chicago Press, 1972), p. 192.
9. Ibid., p. 194.
10. Raymond M. Olderman, *Beyond the Wasteland: The American Novel in the Nineteen-Sixties* (New Haven: Yale University Press, 1972), pp. 2, 6.
11. Robert Scholes, *The Fabulators* (New York: Oxford University Press, 1967), p. 54.
12. Ihab Hassan, *Contemporary Amercian Literature 1945–1972: An Introduction* (New York: Frederick Ungar Press, 1972), p. 25.
13. Philip Roth, "Writing American Fiction," *Commentary*, 31 (March 1961): 224.
14. Alfred Kazin, "Oates," *Harper's*, 243 (Aug. 1971): 81.
15. "Transformations of Self," p. 57.
16. Saul Bellow, "The Writer as Moralist," *Atlantic Monthly*, 209 (March 1963): 62.
17. Oates, "An American Tragedy," p. 12.
18. Joyce Carol Oates, "The Visionary Art of Flannery O'Connor," *Southern Humanities Review*, 7 (Summer 1973): 242.
19. Clemons, p. 77.
20. Joyce Carol Oates, "Swamps," in *By the North Gate* (New York: Vanguard Press, 1963), p. 17.
21. Clemons, p. 77. See also "Transformations of Self," p. 59.

22. Clemons, p. 77.

23. Calvin Bedient, "Vivid and Dazzling," reviews of *them* and *Anonymous Sins, Nation,* 209 (1 Dec. 1969): 610.

24. Walter Sullivan, "The Artificial Demon: Joyce Carol Oates and the Dimensions of the Real," *Hollins Critic,* 9 (Dec. 1972): 12.

25. "Transformations of Self," p. 57.

26. Charles Glicksberg, "The Literature of Silence," *Centennial Review,* 14 (Spring 1970): 169.

27. Kurt Vonnegut, *Cat's Cradle* (New York: Dell, 1968), epigraph.

28. Frank Kermode, *The Sense of an Ending* (New York: Oxford University Press, 1967), p. 103.

29. "Transformations of Self," p. 54.

30. Oates, "An American Tragedy," p. 2.

31. Hassan, p. 27.

32. Scholes, p. 11.

33. Joyce Carol Oates, "Double Tragedy Strikes Tennessee Hill Family," *Carolina Quarterly,* 24 (Winter 1972): 87–99.

34. Anaïs Nin, *The Novel of the Future* (New York: Macmillan, 1968), p. 199.

35. Susan Cornillon, ed., *Images of Women In Fiction* (Bowling Green, Ohio: Bowling Green University Press, 1972), p. 117.

36. Joyce Carol Oates, *Miracle Play* (Los Angeles: Black Sparrow Press, 1974), pp. 86, 8.

37. Granville Hicks, review of *Expensive People, Saturday Review,* 26 Oct. 1968, p. 34.

38. Five of the fourteen stories in *By the North Gate* begin in this way.

39. Joyce Oates Smith, "Ritual and Violence in Flannery O'Connor," *Thought,* 41 (Winter 1966): 547.

40. Oates, "A Visit with Doris Lessing," pp. 881, 878.

41. Joyce Carol Oates, *The Hostile Sun: The Poetry of D. H. Lawrence* (Los Angeles: Black Sparrow Press, 1973), p. 21.

42. Ibid., p. 14.

43. Ibid., p. 24.

44. John L'Heureux, "Mirage-Seekers," *Atlantic,* 224 (Oct. 1969): 128.

45. Oates, "An American Tragedy," p. 2.

46. Ibid.

47. Ibid.

48. "Transformations of Self," p. 53.

49. Ibid., p. 54.

50. Christopher Lehmann-Haupt, "Stalking the Eternal Feminine," *New York Times,* 15 Oct. 1973, p. 35.

51. Mary Ellmann, "Nolo Contendere," *New York Review of Books,* 24 Jan. 1974, p. 37.

52. Oates, "An American Tragedy," p. 2.

53. Ibid.

Chapter two (*pages 31–61*)

1. Joyce Oates Smith, "Ritual and Violence in Flannery O'Connor," *Thought,* 41 (Winter 1966): 547.

2. Rollo May, *Power and Innocence: A Search for the Sources of Violence* (New York: Norton, 1972), pp. 233, 182.

3. J[acob] Bronowski, *The Face of Violence: An Essay with a Play* (New York: World Publishing Co., 1967), pp. 76, 81.

4. Hannah Arendt, "On Violence," in *Crises of the Republic* (New York: Harcourt, Brace, Jovanovich, 1972), p. 160.

5. Erich Fromm, *The Anatomy of Human Destructiveness* (New York: Holt, Rinehart, and Winston, 1973), p. 267.

6. Arendt, pp. 143–45, 155.

7. Jean-Paul Sartre, Preface to Frantz Fanon, *The Wretched of the Earth* (New York: Grove Press, 1963), p. 18. Oates alludes to Fanon's work in *them*; it is a handbook of the revolutionists (*them* 463).

8. Joyce Carol Oates, "The Visionary Art of Flannery O'Connor," *Southern Humanities Review*, 7 (Summer 1973): 236.

9. [Oates], "Ritual and Violence," p. 551.

10. William James, "The Moral Equivalent of War," in Terry Maple, Douglas W. Matheson, eds., *Aggression, Hostility, and Violence* (New York: Holt, Rinehart, and Winston, 1973), p. 258.

11. May, pp. 177, 233.

12. Anaïs Nin, *The Novel of the Future* (New York: Macmillan, 1968), pp. 35, 173.

13. Iris Murdoch, "Against Dryness," *Encounter*, 16 (Jan. 1961): 21.

14. Warren Bower, "Bliss in the First Person," *Saturday Review*, 26 Oct. 1968, p. 33.

15. Martin Heidegger, *Introduction to Metaphysics* (New Haven: Yale University Press, 1968), p. 150.

16. Hans Toch, *Violent Men: An Inquiry into the Psychology of Violence* (Chicago: Aldine Publishing Co., 1969), pp. 135-36.

17. Joyce Carol Oates explains in her introductory remarks to *them* that she learned the facts of the novel from one of her former students. In the novel, she uses her own name, identifying herself as Maureen's teacher.

18. Joyce Carol Oates, "Building Tension in the Short Story," *The Writer*, 79 (June 1966): 12.

19. Elizabeth Dalton, "Joyce Carol Oates: Violence in the Head," *Commentary*, 49 (June 1970): 75.

20. Ibid., p. 77.

21. Ibid., p. 75.

22. Joyce Carol Oates, "An American Tragedy," *New York Times Book Review*, 24 Jan. 1971, p. 2.

Chapter three (*pages 62–92*)

1. Charles Glaab and A. Theodore Brown, *A History of Urban America* (New York: Macmillan, 1967), p. 8.

2. Quoted in Perry Miller, *The American Puritans* (New York: Doubleday, 1956), p. 83.

3. Quoted in Norman Holmes Pearson, "The American Writer and the Feeling for Community," *English Studies*, 43 (Oct. 1962): 403. Source not given.

4. Thomas Ford Hould, ed., *Dictionary of Modern Sociology* (Totowa, N.J.: Littlefield, Adams and Co., 1969), p. 73.

5. Robert Mills French, ed., *The Community: A Comparative Perspective* (Itasca, Ill., F. E. Peacock, 1969), p. 5.

6. Seymour B. Sarason, *The Psychological Sense of Community: Prospects for a Community Psychology* (San Francisco: Jossey-Bass, 1974), p. 1.

7. Richard N. Goodwin, "Reflections: The American Condition II," *New Yorker*, 28 Jan. 1974, pp. 37, 38.

8. Sam Bass Warner, *The Urban Wilderness: A History of the American City* (New York: Harper, 1972), p. 5.

9. Cited in Vance Packard, *A Nation of Strangers* (New York: David McKay, 1972), p. 211.

10. Pearson, p. 403.

11. Packard, p. x.

12. Goodwin, p. 36.

13. See Richard N. Goodwin, "Reflections: The American Condition I," *New Yorker*, 21 Jan. 1974, pp. 39–42.

14. Harvey Cox, *The Seduction of the Spirit* (New York: Simon and Schuster, 1973), p. 90.

15. Kenneth R. Boulding, "The City as an Element in the International System," *Daedalus*, 97 (Fall 1968): p. 1118.

16. Joyce Carol Oates, "New Heaven and Earth," *Saturday Review of the Arts*, 4 Nov. 1972, p. 54.

17. Joyce Carol Oates, "An American Tragedy," *New York Times Book Review*, 24 Jan. 1971, p. 2.

18. William Wordsworth, *The Prelude: A Parallel Text*, ed. J. C. Maxwell (Baltimore: Penguin Books, 1971), p. 286, ll. 592–606.

19. "Conversations with Dan Berrigan on Detroit, survival, and hope," *Detroit Free Press*, 6 April 1975, Detroit sec., p. 17.

20. William Faulkner, *As I Lay Dying* (New York: Random House, 1964), pp. 34-35.

21. Joyce Carol Oates revised the ending of *Wonderland* after the publication of the hardcover edition. This citation occurs in the revised conclusion to the paperbound edition. In the original version, Jesse leads Shelley away from the house where he had found her. She breaks free of him and runs away. He manages to catch up with her, and they get into a small boat tied to the dock. He releases the boat and they drift all night. The next day they are found by the Mounted Police.

Chapter four (*pages 93–116*)

1. Joyce Carol Oates, ed., *Scenes from American Life* (New York: Random House, 1973), p. vii.

2. John Fraser, *Violence in the Arts* (New York: Cambridge University Press, 1974), p. ix.

3. Joyce Carol Oates, "Don Juan's Last Laugh," *Psychology Today*, 8 (Sept. 1974): 10, 12.

4. William Abrahams, "Stories of a Visionary," *Saturday Review: The Society*, 1 (Oct. 1972): 76.

5. An unpublished paper by Ildikó Carrington, prepared for the MLA Seminar on Oates (December 1973), "Borges and Oates: Monsters in *Wonderland*," discusses the gothic and grotesque dimensions of Oates's novel *Wonderland* and relates it to Borges's works as well as Lewis Carroll's.

6. Joyce Carol Oates, "An American Tragedy," *New York Times Book Review*, 24 Jan. 1971, p. 2.

7. Joyce Carol Oates, "Remarks by Joyce Carol Oates Accepting the National Book Award in Fiction for 'them,' " press release from Vanguard Press, March 4, 1970, p. 2.

8. An unpublished paper by Alice Martin, *"Expensive People,"* delivered at the December 1973 MLA Seminar on Oates, compares Oates's use of nausea with that of Jean-Paul Sartre.

9. John L'Heureux, "Mirage-Seekers," *Atlantic*, 224 (Oct. 1969): 128.

Chapter five (*pages* 117–141)

1. Joyce Carol Oates, "An American Tragedy," *New York Times Book Review*, 24 Jan. 1971, p. 12.

2. Joyce Carol Oates, ed., *Scenes from American Life* (New York: Random House, 1973), p. vii.

3. Ibid., p. viii.

4. Franz Kafka, *Diaries*, quoted in Joyce Carol Oates, *New Heaven and New Earth* (New York: Vanguard Press, 1974), epigraph.

5. Miguel de Unamuno, *The Tragic Sense of Life* (London: Macmillan, 1926), p. 17.

6. Ibid., pp. 25–27.

7. Ibid., p. 55.

8. Raymond Williams, *Modern Tragedy* (Stanford: Stanford University Press, 1966), p. 13.

9. Herbert Muller, *The Spirit of Tragedy* (New York: Knopf, 1956), p. 3.

10. Richard B. Sewall, *The Vision of Tragedy* (New Haven: Yale University Press, 1959), pp. 1, 4–5.

11. Friedrich Nietzsche, "Why I Write Such Excellent Books," *Complete Works*, XVII (New York: Macmillan, 1924), p. 73.

12. Nietzsche, " 'Reason' in Philosophy," Ibid., XVI, p. 23.

13. Sewall, p. 7.

14. Nathan Scott, *The Tragic Vision and the Christian Faith* (New York: Association Press, 1957), pp. x, xi.

15. See Paul Ricoeur, *The Symbolism of Evil* (New York: Harper and Row, 1967), pp. 232–78.

16. Oates, "An American Tragedy," p. 2.

17. "Transformations of Self: An Interview with Joyce Carol Oates," *Ohio Review*, 15, (Fall 1973): 55.

18. Sewall, p. 147.

19. Ibid., pp. 5–7.

20. Oates, "An American Tragedy," p. 2.

21. Cited in Joyce Carol Oates, *The Edge of Impossibility: Tragic Forms in Literature* (New York: Vanguard Press, 1974). See also Williams, pp. 37–45.

22. See Linda Kuehl, "An Interview with Joyce Carol Oates," *Commonweal*, 5 Dec. 1969, pp. 307–10.

23. Oates, "An American Tragedy," p. 2.

24. Joyce Carol Oates, "Art: Therapy and Magic," *American Journal*, 1 (3 July 1973): 20n.

25. See particularly: Calvin Bedient, review of *Do With Me What You Will*, *New York Times Book Review*, 14 Oct. 1973, pp. 1, 18; Walter Clemons, "Sleeping Princess," *Newsweek*, 15 Oct. 1973, p. 107; Martha Duffy, "Power Vacuum," *Time*, 15 Oct. 1973, p. 126; Mary Ellmann," "Nolo Contendere," *New York Review of Books*, 24 Jan. 1974, pp. 36–37.

26. Alfred Kazin, "Oates," *Harper's*, 243 (Aug. 1971): 81–82.

27. Bedient, p. 18.

28. Joyce Carol Oates, *Poisoned Kiss*, quoted in Elizabeth Pochoda, review of *The Seduction and Other Stories* and *The Poisoned Kiss*, *New York Times Book Review*, 31 Aug. 1975, p. 6.

29. Oates, *Scenes from American Life*, p. vii.

30. Joyce Carol Oates, *Love and Its Derangements* (Baton Rouge, La.: Louisiana State University Press, 1970), p. 24.

31. Oates, "Art: Therapy and Magic," p. 17.

Bibliography

This bibliography represents only those writings of Joyce Carol Oates pertinent to the study of her tragic vision. It is by no means exhaustive. Also not included in the bibliography are those sources quoted in the text and identified in full in the notes, which would have no direct bearing on further study of this topic.

I. Works by Joyce Carol Oates

Novels

Do With Me What You Will. New York: Vanguard Press, 1973.
Expensive People. New York: Vanguard Press, 1968.
A Garden of Earthly Delights. New York: Vanguard Press, 1967.
them. New York: Vanguard Press, 1969.
With Shuddering Fall. New York: Vanguard Press, 1964.
Wonderland. New York: Vanguard Press, 1971; Greenwich, Conn.: Fawcett, 1973. [Author's revised ending.]

Collected short stories

By the North Gate. New York: Vanguard Press, 1963.
The Goddess and Other Women. New York: Vanguard Press, 1974.
The Hungry Ghosts: Seven Allusive Comedies. Los Angeles: Black Sparrow Press, 1974.
Marriages and Infidelities. New York: Vanguard Press, 1972.
The Poisoned Kiss and Other Stories from the Portuguese. New York: Vanguard Press, 1975. (Co-"authored" by Fernandes)

The Seduction and Other Stories. Los Angeles: Black Sparrow Press, 1975.
Upon the Sweeping Flood. New York: Vanguard Press, 1966.
The Wheel of Love and Other Stories. New York: Vanguard Press, 1970.

Collected poems and miscellany

Angel Fire. Baton Rouge, La.: Louisiana State University Press, 1973.
Anonymous Sins and Other Poems. Baton Rouge, La.: Louisiana State University Press, 1969.
"Double Tragedy Strikes Tennessee Hill Family," *Carolina Quarterly,* 24 (Winter 1972): 87–99.
Dreaming America and Other Poems. [n.p.]: Aloe Editions, 1973.
In Case of Accidental Death. Cambridge, Mass.: Pomegranate Press, 1972.
Love and Its Derangements. Baton Rouge, La.: Louisiana State University Press, 1970.
Miracle Play. Los Angeles: Black Sparrow Press, 1974.
Plagiarized Material by Fernandes "Translated" by Joyce Carol Oates. Los Angeles: Black Sparrow Press, 1974.
A Posthumous Sketch. Los Angeles: Black Sparrow Press, 1973.
"Remarks by Joyce Carol Oates Accepting the National Book Award in Fiction for 'them.' " Press release, Vanguard Press, March 4, 1970.
Scenes from American Life: Contemporary Short Fiction. Edited by Oates. New York: Random House, 1973.
Women in Love and Other Poems. New York: Albondacani Press, 1968.
Wooded Forms. New York: Albondacani Press, 1972.

Critical essays

"Art: Therapy and Magic." *American Journal* 1 (3 July 1973): 17–20.
"Background and Foreground in Fiction." *The Writer* 80 (Aug. 1967): 11–13.
"Building Tensions in the Short Story." *The Writer* 79 (June 1966): 11–12, 44.
The Edge of Impossibility: Tragic Forms in Literature. New York: Vanguard Press, 1972.

"The Myth of the Isolated Artist." *Psychology Today* 6 (May 1973):
  74–75.
"New Heaven and Earth," *Saturday Review of the Arts*, 4 Nov. 1972,
  pp. 51–54.
New Heaven, New Earth: The Visionary Experience in Literature.
  New York: Vanguard Press, 1974.
"The Short Story." *Southern Humanities Review* 5 (Summer, 1971):
  213–14.
"The Unique / Universal in Fiction." *Techniques of Novel Writing.*
  Ed. A. S. Burdack. Boston: The Writer, Inc., 1973, pp. 71–77.

On other authors

"An American Tragedy." *New York Times Book Review*, 24 Jan. 1971,
  pp. 2, 12, 14, 16.
"The Art of Eudora Welty." *Shenandoah* 20, No. 3 (1969): 54–57.
"The Death Throes of Romanticism: The Poems of Sylvia Plath."
  Southern Review 9 (July 1973): 501–22.
"Don Juan's Last Laugh." Review of *Tales of Power* by Carlos Cas-
  taneda. *Psychology Today* 8 (Sept. 1974): 10, 12, 130.
The Hostile Sun: The Poetry of D. H. Lawrence. Los Angeles: Black
  Sparrow Press, 1973.
" 'The Immense Indifference of Things': The Tragedy of *Nostromo*."
  Novel 9 (Fall 1975): 5–22.
"Man Under the Sentence of Death: The Novels of James M. Cain."
  In *Tough Guys of the Thirties*, edited by David Madden. Carbon-
  dale, Ill.: Southern Illinois University Press, 1968, pp. 110–28.
"A Personal View of Nabokov." *Saturday Review of the Arts*, Jan.
  1973, pp. 36–37.
"Ritual and Violence in Flannery O'Connor." *Thought* 41 (Winter
  1966): 545–60. [This appeared with signature: Joyce Oates
  Smith.]
"The Teleology of the Unconscious: The Art of Norman Mailer."
  Critic 32 (Nov.–Dec. 1973): 25–35.
"With Norman Mailer at the Sex Circus: II Out of the Machine."
  Atlantic 228 (July 1971): 42–45.
"The Visionary Art of Flannery O'Connor." *Southern Humanities
  Review* 7 (Summer 1973): 235–46.
"A Visit with Doris Lessing." *Southern Review* 9 (Oct. 1973): 873–
  82.

II. Works about Joyce Carol Oates

Interviews, biographical studies, reviews

Abrahams, William. "Stories of a Visionary." Review of *Marriages &
Infidelities*. *Saturday Review: The Society* 1 (Oct. 1972): 76–78.
Bedient, Calvin. Review of *Do With Me What You Will*. *New York
Times Book Review* 14 Oct. 1973, pp. 1, 18.
———. "Vivid and Dazzling." *Nation*, 1 Dec. 1969, pp. 609–11.
Bellamy, Joe David. "The Dark Lady of American Letters: An Inter-
view with Joyce Carol Oates." *Atlantic* 229 (Feb. 1972): 63–67.
Bower, Warren. "Bliss in the First Person." *Saturday Review*, 26 Oct.
1968, pp. 33–34.
Clemons, Walter. "Joyce Carol Oates at Home." *New York Times
Book Review*, 28 Sept. 1969, pp. 4, 5, 48.
———. "Joyce Carol Oates: Love and Violence."*Newsweek*, 11 Dec.
1972, pp. 72–77.
———. "Sleeping Princess." Review of *Do With Me What You Will*.
Newsweek, 15 Oct. 1973, p. 107.
Dalton, Elizabeth. "Joyce Carol Oates: Violence in the Head." *Com-
mentary* 49 (June 1970): 75–77.
de Ramus, Betty. "Peeking into the Very Private World of Joyce Carol
Oates." *Detroit Free Press*, 3 March 1974, Detroit Section, pp.
13–15.
Duffy, Martha. "Power Vacuum." Review of *Do With Me What You
Will*. *Time*, 15 Oct. 1973, p. 126.
Duus, Louise. " 'The Population of Eden': Joyce Carol Oates's *By the
North Gate*." *Critique* 7 (Winter 1964): 176–77.
Ellmann, Mary. "*Nolo Contendere*." Review of *Do With Me What
You Will*. *New York Review of Books*, 24 Jan. 1974, pp. 36–37.
Engel, Marian. "Women also have dark hearts." Review of *The Goddess
and Other Women*. *New York Times Book Review*, 24 Nov. 1974,
pp. 7, 10.
Hardwick, Elizabeth. "Reflections on Fiction." *New York Review of
Books*, 13 Feb. 1969, p. 16.
Hendin, Josephine. "Joyce Carol Oates is frankly murderous." Review
of *The Hungry Ghosts*. *New York Times Book Review*, 1 Sept.
1974, p. 5.
Hicks, Granville. Review of *Expensive People*. *Saturday Review*, 26
Oct. 1968, pp. 33–34.
Kazin, Alfred. "Oates." *Harper's* 243 (Aug. 1971): 78–82.

Knowles, John. "Nada at the Core." Review of *Expensive People. New York Times Book Review*, 3 Nov. 1968, p. 4.

——. "A Racing Car Is the Symbol of Violence." Review of *With Shuddering Fall. New York Times Book Review*, 25 Oct. 1964, p. 5.

Kuehl, Linda. "An Interview with Joyce Carol Oates." *Commonweal*, 5 Dec. 1969, pp. 307–10.

Lehmann-Haupt, Christopher. "Stalking the Eternal Feminine." *New York Times*, 15 Oct. 1973, p. 35.

L'Heureux, John. "Mirage-Seekers." Review of *them. Atlantic* 224 (Oct. 1969): 128–29.

——. "Something New, Something Blue." Review of *Expensive People. Critic* 27 (Feb.–March, 1969): 83–85.

Pochoda, Elizabeth. "Joyce Carol Oates honoring the complexities of the real world." Review of *The Seduction and Other Stories* and *The Poisoned Kiss. New York Times Book Review*, 31 Aug. 1975, p. 6.

Sullivan, Walter. "Where Have All the Flowers Gone?: The Short Story in Search of Itself." *Sewanee Review*, 78 (Summer 1970): 531–42.

"Transformation of Self: An Interview with Joyce Carol Oates." *Ohio Review*, 15, No. 1 (Fall 1973): 51–61.

"Urban Gothic." Review of *them. Time*, 10 Oct. 1969, pp. 106–8.

Wolff, Geoffrey. "Gothic City." Review of *them. Newsweek*, 29 Sept. 1969, p. 120.

——. "Wonderland." *New York Times Book Review*, 24 Oct. 1971, p. 5.

"Writing as a Natural Reaction." *Time*, 10 Oct. 1969, p. 108.

Studies on Oates

Berets, Ralph. "Joyce Carol Oates's *Wonderland* Seen as a Mythic Rite of Passage." Seminar paper. MLA, 1973.

Burwell, Rose Marie. "Joyce Carol Oates and an Old Master." *Critique*, 15, No. 1 (1974): 48–58.

Carrington, Ildikó. "Borges and Oates: Monsters in *Wonderland*." Seminar paper. MLA, 1973.

"Conversations with Dan Berrigan on Detroit, survival and hope." *Detroit Free Press*, 6 April 1975, *Detroit* section, pp. 17–21.

Giles, James R. "From Jimmy Gatz to Jules Wendall: A Study in 'Nothing Substantial.'" Seminar paper. MLA, 1973.

Harter, Carol. "America as 'Consumer Garden': The Nightmare Vision of Joyce Carol Oates." Paper presented at Ohio-Indiana American Studies Meeting, Spring 1974.

Kazin, Alfred. "Cassandras: Porter to Oates." *Bright Book of Life: American Novelists and Storytellers from Hemingway to Mailer.* Boston: Little, Brown and Co., 1973, pp. 163-206.

Martin, Alice. "*Expensive People*, 1968." Seminar paper. MLA, 1973.

Pinsker, Sanford. "Isaac Bashevis Singer and Joyce Carol Oates: Some Versions of Gothic." *Southern Review* 9 (Oct. 1973): 895–908.

Sullivan, Walter. "The Artificial Demon: Joyce Carol Oates and the Dimensions of the Real." *The Hollins Critic* 9 (Dec. 1972).

Walker, Carolyn. "Fear, Love, and Art in Oates's 'Plot.'" *Critique* 15, No. 1 (1974): 59–70.

Wegs, Joyce M. "'Do You Know Who I Am?': The Grotesque in Oates's 'Where Are You Going, Where Have You Been?'" Seminar paper. MLA, 1973.

———. "The Grotesque in Some Novels of the Nineteen-Sixties: Ken Kesey, Joyce Carol Oates, Sylvia Plath." Ph.D. dissertation, University of Illinois, 1973.

III. General Background

Community, city, violence

Arendt, Hannah. "On Violence." *Crises of the Republic.* New York: Harcourt, Brace, Jovanovich, 1972, pp. 105–98.

Baltzel, E. Digby, ed. *The Search for Community in Modern America.* New York: Harper and Row, 1968.

Banfield, Edward C. *The Unheavenly City: The Nature and Future of Our Urban Crisis.* Boston: Little, Brown, 1970.

Bell, Daniel. *The Coming of Post-Industrial Society.* New York: Basic Books, 1973.

Berdyaev, Nikolai. *The Fate of Man in the Modern World.* Translated by Donald A. Lowrie. Ann Arbor: Ann Arbor Paperbacks, 1935.

———. *Slavery and Freedom.* Translated by R. M. French. New York: Charles Scribner's Sons, 1944.

Boulding, Kenneth. "The City as an Element in the International System." *Daedalus* 97 (Fall 1968): 1111–23.

Brindenbaugh, Carl. *Cities in the Wilderness.* New York: Knopf, 1960.

Bronowski, J[acob]. *The Face of Violence: An Essay with a Play.* New York: World Publishing, 1967.

Cox, Harvey. *The Secular City.* Rev. ed. New York: Macmillan, 1966.

————. *The Seduction of the Spirit: The Use and Misuse of People's Religion*. New York: Simon and Schuster, 1973.

de Grazia, Sebastian. *The Political Community: A Study in Anomie*. Chicago: University of Chicago Press, 1948.

Ellul, Jacques. *The Meaning of the City*. Grand Rapids, Mich.: Eerdmans, 1970.

————. *Violence: Reflections from a Christian Perspective*. Translated by Cecilia Gaul Kings. New York: Seabury Press, 1969.

Fraser, John. *Violence in the Arts*. New York: Cambridge University Press, 1974.

French, Robert Mills, ed. *The Community: A Comparative Perspective*. Itasca, Ill.: F. E. Peacock, 1969.

Fromm, Erich. *The Anatomy of Human Destructiveness*. New York: Holt, Rinehart, 1973.

Geen, Elizabeth, Jeanne R. Lowe, and Kenneth Walker, eds. *Man and the Modern City*. Pittsburgh: University of Pittsburgh Press, 1963.

————. *The American City: A Documentary History*. Homewood, Ill.: Dorsey Press, 1966.

Glaab, Charles and A. Theodore Brown. *A History of Urban America*. New York: Macmillan, 1967.

Glazer, Nathan and Daniel Patrick Moynihan. *Beyond the Melting Pot*. Cambridge: Harvard University Press, 1963.

Goist, Park Dixon. "City and 'Community': Urban Theory of Robert Park." *American Quarterly* 23 (Spring 1971): 46–59.

————. "Town, City, and 'Community' 1890–1920's." *American Studies*, 14 (Spring 1973): 15–28.

Goodman, Paul. *Growing Up Absurd: Problems of Youth in the Organized System*. New York: Random House, 1960.

————. *Empire City*. Indianapolis: Bobbs-Merrill, 1959.

Goodman, Paul, and Percival Goodman. *Communitas: Means of Livelihood and Ways of Life*. Chicago: University of Chicago Press, 1947.

Goodwin, Richard N. "Reflections: The American Condition." I, *New Yorker*, 21 Jan. 1974, pp. 35-60; II, *New Yorker*, 28 Jan. 1974, pp. 36–68; III, *New Yorker*, 4 Feb. 1974, pp. 48–91.

Green, Constance McLaughlin. *American Cities in the Growth of the Nation*. New York: Harper and Row, 1957.

Greer, Scott. *The Emerging City: Myth and Reality*. Glencoe, Ill.: Free Press, 1962.

Hays, Hoffman Reynolds. *The Dangerous Sex: The Myth of Feminine Evil*. New York: Putnam's, 1964.

Jacobs, Jane. *The Death and Life of Great American Cities*. New York: Random House, 1961.

James, William. "The Moral Equivalent of War." In Terry Maple and Douglas M. Matheson, eds., *Aggression, Hostility. and Violence: Nature or Nurture.* New York: Holt, Rinehart, and Winston, 1973, pp. 258–62.

Janeway, Elizabeth. *Man's World, Woman's Place: A Study in Social Mythology.* New York: Morrow, 1971.

————, ed. *Women: Their Changing Roles.* New York: Arno Press, 1973.

Jeffrey, Kirk. "The Family as Utopian Retreat from the City." *Soundings,* 15 (Spring 1972): 21–41.

Jones, Howard Mumford. *Violence and the Humanist.* Middlebury, Vt.: Middlebury College, 1967.

Kaul, A. N. *The American Vision: Actual and Ideal Society in Nineteenth-Century Fiction.* New Haven: Yale University Press, 1963.

Keniston, Kenneth. *The Uncommitted: Alienated Youth in American Society.* New York: Harcourt, 1965.

Keyes, Ralph. *We, the Lonely People.* New York: Harper and Row, 1973.

Koenig, Rene. *The Community.* Translated by Edward Fitzgerald. New York: Humanities Press, 1968.

Lynch, Kevin. *The Image of the City.* Cambridge: Harvard University Press, 1969.

McDermott, John J. "Nature Nostalgia and the City." *Soundings* 15 (Spring 1972): 1–19.

McHarg, Ian. *Design with Nature.* Garden City, N.Y.: The Natural History Press, 1969.

McWilliams, Wilson Carey. *The Idea of Fraternity in America.* Berkeley: University of California Press, 1973.

Marx, Leo. *The Machine in the Garden: Technology and the Pastoral Idea in America.* New York: Oxford University Press, 1964.

May, Rollo. *Power and Innocence: A Search for the Sources of Violence.* New York: Norton, 1972.

Millett, Kate, *Sexual Politics.* New York: Avon, 1970.

Minar, David W., and Scott Greer, eds. *Concept of Community: Readings with Interpretations.* Chicago: Aldine, 1969.

Mumford, Lewis. *The City in History: Its Origins, Its Transformations, and Its Prospects.* New York: Harcourt, 1961.

————. *The Culture of Cities.* New York: Harcourt, 1938.

Nisbet, Robert A. *The Quest for Community.* New York: Oxford University Press, 1953.

————. *The Sociological Tradition: Readings in Urban Sociology.* New York: Basic Books, 1966.

Packard, Vance. *Nation of Strangers.* New York: David McKay, 1972.

Park, Robert E. *Human Communities*. Glencoe, Ill.: Free Press, 1952.
———, Ernest W. Burgess, and Roderick D. McKenzie. *The City*. Chicago: University of Chicago Press, 1967.
Pierson, George W. *The Moving American*. New York: Knopf, 1973.
Reeves, Nancy. *Womankind: Beyond the Stereotypes*. Chicago: Aldine-Atherton, 1971.
Reichert, William O. "Woman, Violence, and Social Order in America." *Centennial Review*, 15 (Winter 1971): 1–22.
Reik, Theodor. *The Creation of Eve*. New York: McGraw-Hill, 1960.
Reische, Diana. *Woman and Society*. New York: Wilson, 1972.
Reps, John W. *The Making of Urban America: A History of City Planning in the United States*. Princeton, N.J.: Princeton University Press, 1965.
Ricoeur, Paul. *The Symbolism of Evil*. Translated by Emerson Buchanan. New York: Harper and Row, 1967.
Riesman, David, Nathan Glazer, and Renee Denney. *The Lonely Crowd: A Study in the Changing American Character*. New Haven: Yale University Press, 1950.
Rowbothan, Sheila. *Women, Resistance, and Revolution*. New York: Random House, 1972.
Royce, Josiah. "The Hope of the Great Community." *The Hope of the Great Community*. New York: Macmillan, 1916, pp. 25–70.
Roszak, Theodore. *Where the Wasteland Ends: Politics and Transcendence in Post-Industrial Society*. New York: Doubleday, 1973.
Saranson, Seymour B. *The Psychological Sense of Community: Prospects for a Community Psychology*. San Francisco: Jossey-Bass, 1974.
Sartre, Jean-Paul. Preface to Frantz Fanon, *The Wretched of the Earth*. Translated by Constance Farrington. New York: Grove Press, 1963, pp. 7–26.
Schlesinger, Arthur M. *The Rise of the City*. New York: Macmillan, 1933.
Schlesinger, Arthur M., Jr. *Violence: America in the Sixties*. New York: Signet, 1968.
Schmitt, Peter J. *Back to Nature: The Arcadian Myth in Urban America*. New York: Oxford University Press, 1969.
Slater, Philip. *The Pursuit of Loneliness: American Culture at the Breaking Point*. Boston: Beacon Press, 1970.
Smith, Page. "*As a City upon a Hill*": *The Town in American History*. New York: Knopf, 1966.
———. *Daughters of the Promised Land: Women in American History*. Boston: Little, Brown, 1970.
Stein, Maurice. *The Eclipse of Community*. New York: Harper, 1964.

Stern, Paula. "The Womanly Image: Character Assassination Through the Ages." *Atlantic* 229 (March 1970): 87–90.
Strauss, Anselm. *Images of the American City*. New York: Free Press, 1961.
Suttie, Ian D. *The Origins of Love and Hate*. New York: The Julian Press, 1966.
Swanson, Bert E. *The Concern for Community in Urban America*. New York: Odyssey Press, 1970.
Tiger, Lionel. *Men in Groups*. New York: Random House, 1969.
Toch, Hans. *Violent Men: An Inquiry into the Psychology of Violence*. Chicago: Aldine Publishing Co., 1969.
Vidich, Arthur J., Joseph Mensman, and Maurice Stein. *Reflections on Community Studies*. New York: Wiley, 1964.
Warner, Sam Bass. *The Private City: Philadelphia in Three Periods of Its Growth*. Philadelphia: University of Pennsylvania Press, 1970.
————. *Streetcar Suburbs: The Process of Growth in Boston 1870–1900*. Cambridge: Harvard University Press, 1962.
————. *The Urban Wilderness: A History of the American City*. New York: Harper, 1972.
Warren, Roland L. *The Community in America*. Chicago: Rand McNally, 1972.
Weber, Max. *The City*. New York: Free Press, 1958.
White, Lucian and Morton White. *The Intellectual Versus the City*. Cambridge: Harvard University Press, 1962.
Wirth, Louis. "Urbanism as a Way of Life." In *Reader in Urban Sociology*, edited by Paul Hatt and Albert Reiss. Glencoe, Ill.: Free Press, 1951, pp. 32–49.

Literary theory

Arden, Eugene. "The Evil City in American Fiction." *New York History* 35 (July 1954): 259–79.
Bergonzi, Bernard. *The Situation of the Novel*. London: Macmillan, 1971.
Berthoff, Warner. *Fiction and Events: Essays in Criticism and Literary History*. New York: Dutton, 1971.
Blotner, Joseph. "The Role of Women." *The Modern American Political Novel*. Austin, Texas: University of Texas Press, 1966, pp. 164-90.
Cornillon, Susan Koppelman, ed. *Images of Women in Fiction*. Bowling Green, Ohio: Bowling Green University, Popular Press, 1972.
Corrigan, Robert W., ed. *Tragedy: Vision and Form*. San Francisco: Chandler Publishing Co., 1963.

Deegan, Dorothy Yost. *The Stereotype of the Single Woman in American Novels.* New York: King's Crown Press, Columbia University, 1951.

Dunlap, George. *The City in the American Novel 1789–1900.* New York: Russell and Russell, 1965.

Earle, William. "Being Versus Tragedy." *Chicago Review* 14 (Autumn-Winter 1960): 107–14.

Ellman, Mary. *Thinking about Women.* New York: Harcourt, 1968.

Ferguson, Mary Anne. *Images of Women in Literature.* Boston: Houghton Mifflin, 1973.

Fiedler, Leslie. *Love and Death in the American Novel.* Rev. ed. New York: Dell, 1966.

Frohock, W. M. *The Novel of Violence in America.* Rev. ed. Dallas: Southern Methodist University Press, 1957.

Gass, William. *Fiction and the Figures of Life.* New York: Knopf, 1970.

Gelfant, Blanche H. *The American City Novel.* Norman, Okla.: University of Oklahoma Press, 1954.

Glicksberg, Charles I. "The Literature of Silence," *Centennial Review* 14 (Spring 1970): 166–76.

———. *The Sexual Revolution in Modern American Literature.* The Hague: Martinus Nijhoff, 1971.

———. *The Tragic Vision in Twentieth-Century Literature.* New York: Dell, 1963.

Goldknopf, David. *The Life of the Novel.* Chicago: University of Chicago Press, 1972.

Gossett, Louise Y. *Violence in Recent Southern Fiction.* Durham, N.C.: Duke University Press, 1965.

Gould, James A. and John J. Iorio. *Violence in Modern Literature.* San Francisco: Boyd and Fraser, 1972.

Grossvogel, David I. *Limits of the Novel: Evolutions of a Form from Chaucer to Robbe-Grillet.* Ithaca, N.Y.: Cornell University Press, 1968.

Hall, Robert W. "Being and Tragedy." *Chicago Review* 14 (Autumn-Winter 1960): 99–106.

Hassan, Ihab. *Contemporary American Literature, 1945–1972: An Introduction.* New York: Frederick Ungar Press, 1973.

———. *The Dismemberment of Orpheus: Towards Postmodern Literature.* New York: Oxford University Press, 1971.

———. *Liberations: New Essays on Humanities in Revolution.* Middletown, Conn.: Wesleyan University Press, 1971.

———. *Radical Innocence: The Contemporary American Novel.* New York: Harper, 1961.

Kaufmann, Walter. *Tragedy and Philosophy*. Garden City, N.Y.: Doubleday and Co., 1969.

Kermode, Frank. *The Sense of an Ending: Studies in the Theory of Fiction*. New York: Oxford University Press, 1967.

Klein, Marcus. *After Alienation*. New York: World, 1964.

Kreiger, Murray. *The Tragic Vision*. New York: Holt, Rinehart, and Winston, 1960.

Krook, Dorothea. *The Elements of Tragedy*. New Haven: Yale University Press, 1969.

Lange, Victor. "Fact in Fiction." *Comparative Literature Studies* 6 (Sept. 1969): 253–61.

Levin, Harry. "From Gusle to Tape Recorder." *Comparative Literature Studies* 6 (Sept. 1969): 262–73.

Lodge, David. *The Language of Fiction: Essays in Criticism and Verbal Analysis of the English Novel*. New York: Columbia University Press, 1967.

————. *The Novelist at the Crossroads and Other Essays on Fiction and Criticism*. Ithaca, N.Y.: Cornell University Press, 1971.

Martin, Wendy. "Seduced and Abandoned in the New World: The Image of Woman in American Fiction." *Woman in Sexist Society*, edited by Vivian Garnick and Barbara K. Moran. New York: Basic Books, 1971, pp. 226–39.

Miller, James E., Jr. *Quests Surd and Absurd: Essays in American Fiction*. Chicago: University of Chicago Press, 1967.

Miller, Joseph Hillis, ed. *Aspects of Narrative*. New York: Columbia University Press, 1971.

Muller, Herbert. *The Spirit of Tragedy*. New York: Knopf, 1956.

Murdoch, Iris. "Against Dryness." *Encounter* 16 (Jan. 1961): 16–20.

Nietzsche, Friedrich. *The Birth of Tragedy and the Genealogy of Morals*. Translated by Golffing. Garden City, N.Y.: Doubleday, 1956.

————. " 'Reason' in Philosophy." *Complete Works*, XVI. New York: Macmillan, 1924.

————. "Why I Write Such Excellent Books." *Complete Works*, XVII. New York: Macmillan, 1924.

Nin, Anaïs. *The Novel of the Future*. New York: Macmillan, 1968.

Noble, David W. *The Eternal Adam and the New World Garden*. New York: Grosset and Dunlap, 1968.

Olderman, Raymond M. *Beyond the Wasteland: The American Novel in the Nineteen-Sixties*. New Haven: Yale University Press, 1972.

Pearson, Norman Holmes. "The American Writer and the Feeling for Community." *English Studies* 43 (Oct. 1962): 403–12.

Raphael, D[avid] D. *The Paradox of Tragedy*. Bloomington, Ind.: Indiana University Press, 1960.

Reiner, Margit. "The Fictional American Woman." *Masses and Mainstream* 5 (June 1952): 1–16.

Robbe-Grillet, Alain. *For a New Novel: Essays on Fiction*. New York: Grove Press, 1965.

Rogers, Katharine M. *Troublesome Helpmate: A History of Misogyny in Literature*. Seattle: University of Washington Press, 1966.

Rose, Alan Henry. "Sin and the City: The Uses of Disorder in the Urban Novel." *Centennial Review* 16 (Summer 1972): 203–20.

Roth, Philip. "Writing American Fiction." *Commentary* 31 (March 1961): 222–33.

Rubin, Louis D., ed. *The Curious Death of the Novel*. Baton Rouge, La.: Louisiana State University Press, 1967.

Rupp, Richard H. *Celebration in Postwar American Fiction*. Coral Gables, Fla.: University of Miami Press, 1970.

Scholes, Robert. *The Fabulators*. New York: Oxford University Press, 1967.

———— and Robert Kellogg. *The Nature of Narrative*. New York: Oxford University Press, 1966.

Scott, Nathan A., Jr. "The Broken Center: A Definition of the Crisis of Values in Modern Literature." *Symbolism in Religion and Literature*, edited by Rollo May. New York: George Braziller, 1960, pp. 178–202.

————. *The Tragic Vision and The Christian Faith*. New York: Association Press, 1957.

Sewall, Richard B. *The Vision of Tragedy*. New Haven: Yale University Press, 1959.

Steiner, George. *The Death of Tragedy*. New York: Knopf, 1961.

Stevick, Philip. *The Theory of the Novel*. New York: Free Press, 1967.

"Symposium: Violence in Literature." Theodore Solotaroff, Robert Penn Warren, Robert Coles, and William Styron. *American Scholar* 37 (Summer 1968): 482–96.

Tanner, Tony. *City of Words: American Fiction, 1950–1970*. London: Jonathan Cape, 1971.

Trilling, Diana. "The Image of Women in Contemporary Literature." *The Woman in America*, edited by Robert Jay Lifton. Boston: Beacon Press, 1965, pp. 52–71.

Unamuno, Miguel de. *The Tragic Sense of Life*. London: Macmillan, 1926.

Weimar, David R. *The City as a Metaphor*. New York: Random House, 1966.

Williams, Raymond. *Modern Tragedy*. Stanford: Stanford University Press, 1966.

IV. Bibliography

McCormick, Lucienne P. "A Bibliography of Works by and about Joyce Carol Oates." *American Literature* 43 (Winter 1971): 124–32.

Appendix

Remarks by Joyce Carol Oates accepting the National Book Award in Fiction for "them."

Writing fiction today sometimes seems an exercise in stubbornness and an anachronistic gesture that goes against the shrill demands of the age—that only the present has meaning, that the contemplative life is irrelevant, that only the life of purest sensation is divine, and that the act of giving shape to sensation, of giving a permanence to the present, is somehow an inversion of the life principle itself. But writers of prose are tough, meticulous people, dedicated to a systematic analysis of the life of sensation and of the electronic paradise that threatens to make language itself obsolete. Writers of prose are all historians, dealing with the past. It is the legendary quality of the past we are most interested in, the immediate past, mysterious and profound, that feeds into the future. It is writers who create history.

Today, there is a demand that the past be obliterated. The style of the new decade is accelerated and deathly; all this emphasis upon sensation, upon a life altered by various drugs, is a speeding up of the ordinary process of life. It is a gravitation toward death. And inherent in the new generation's rejection of the past is a rejection of the future, a rejection of any extended period of time. This is all deathly, an unconscious desire for death, for the end of consciousness. The artists of America must resist the temptation to give up

The following appendix appears with the author's permission.

[163]

the struggle for consciousness, to go down with the age. It is very tempting for us, this disavowal of intelligence, this sub-religious gesture of surrender to the sense and emotions, to death. Writers of prose and poetry are living in the most stimulating of times today —if only they can survive.

Those of us who are also university teachers can see clearly, in some of our best students, the dangers of the new religion, of the ethic of the unconsciousness: a certain aimlessness, a distrust, a fear of the future that seems to them either forbidding or unimaginable. Many of these students are both older and younger than they should be—older because they have experienced a great deal, younger because the experiences seem to have flowed through them, meaning nothing. It is a mysterious age, the present. It questions all meaning. Writers, trying to make sense of the age, are also creating it, and there is more need than ever for the contemplative life, for an assessment of where we are going and where we have come from. We need to withdraw from the age, to make ourselves detached. The writer of prose is committed to re-creating the world through language, and he should not be distracted from this task by even the most attractive of temptations. The opposite of language is silence; silence for human beings is death.

In the novels I have written, I have tried to give a shape to certain obsessions of mid-century Americans—a confusion of love and money, of the categories of public and private experience, of a demonic urge I sense all around me, an urge to violence as the answer to all problems, an urge to self-annihilation, suicide, the ultimate experience and the ultimate surrender. The use of language is all we have to pit against death and silence.

Index

[166]